Shifting From
Me to We

How to Jump-Start Collaboration in a PLC at Work®

MICHAEL ROBERTS

Solution Tree | Press

a division of
Solution Tree

555 North Morton Street
Bloomington, IN 47404
800.733.6786 (toll free) / 812.336.7700
FAX: 812.336.7790

email: info@SolutionTree.com
SolutionTree.com

Visit **go.SolutionTree.com/PLCbooks** to download the free reproducibles in this book.
Printed in the United States of America

Library of Congress Cataloging-in-Publication Data

Names: Roberts, Michael, 1970- author.
Title: Shifting from me to we : how to jump-start collaboration in a PLC at
  work / by Michael Roberts.
Description: Bloomington, IN : Solution Tree Press, 2020. | Includes
  bibliographical references and index.
Identifiers: LCCN 2020003656 (print) | LCCN 2020003657 (ebook) | ISBN
  9781949539851 (Paperback) | ISBN 9781949539868 (eBook)
Subjects: LCSH: Professional learning communities. | Teachers--Professional
  relationships. | Teacher-administrator relationships.
Classification: LCC LB1731 .R563 2020 (print) | LCC LB1731 (ebook) | DDC
  370.71/1--dc23
LC record available at https://lccn.loc.gov/2020003656
LC ebook record available at https://lccn.loc.gov/2020003657

Solution Tree
Jeffrey C. Jones, CEO
Edmund M. Ackerman, President

Solution Tree Press
President and Publisher: Douglas M. Rife
Associate Publisher: Sarah Payne-Mills
Art Director: Rian Anderson
Managing Production Editor: Kendra Slayton
Production Editor: Laurel Hecker
Content Development Specialist: Amy Rubenstein
Copy Editor: Kate St. Ives
Proofreader: Mark Hain
Editorial Assistants: Sarah Ludwig and Elijah Oates

Acknowledgments

It's funny how a moment in an otherwise ordinary day can suddenly change the course of one's life. I was in my office at Housel Middle School, doing something routine, when Deanna Flores walked in and said, "Have you read this?" I hadn't.

This was *Whatever It Takes: How Professional Learning Communities Respond When Kids Don't Learn* by Richard DuFour, Rebecca DuFour, Robert Eaker, and Gayle Karhanek. I consumed it over a weekend and instantly my thoughts of what educators could and should do to support all students changed.

A few weeks later, Mrs. Flores trusted her assistant principal to lead a team of teachers to see Rick and Becky DuFour talk on a stage for two days in Pasco, Washington, and my professional life has never been the same.

Thank you, Deanna. Without that moment, this book never gets started.

I also need to say thank you to:

- Brolin, Quade, and Remy—thank you for being willing to share my time and attention with thousands of children you will never meet. You will always be the students I think of first. I wish for you endless possibilities.

- The amazing educators who generously gave their time to be interviewed to make this book happen.

- The entire Solution Tree family. I cannot tell you how much I have enjoyed working and laughing with you. You are the best.

Solution Tree Press would like to thank the following reviewers:

Brian Greeney
Assistant Superintendent of Innovation, Teaching, and Learning
Willis Independent School District
Willis, Texas

Erica Hidalgo
Director of Elementary Programs
Los Lunas Schools
Los Lunas, New Mexico

Visit **go.SolutionTree.com/PLCbooks** to download the free reproducibles in this book.

Table of Contents

Reproducibles are in italics.

About the Author

 **Michael Roberts** is an author and consultant with more than two decades of experience in education. Michael has been an administrator at the district level and has served as an on-site administrator at the high school, middle school, and elementary levels.

Prior to his stint as the director of elementary curriculum and instruction in Scottsdale, Arizona, Michael was the principal of Desert View Elementary School (DVES) in Hermiston, Oregon. Under his leadership, DVES produced evidence of increased learning each year from 2013 to 2017 for all students and met the challenges of 40 percent growth over four years, a rising population of English learners, and a dramatic increase in the number of trauma-affected students. Michael attributes the success of DVES to the total commitment of staff to the three big ideas and the four critical questions of a professional learning community. This commitment has led to a schoolwide transition from *me* to *we*—a fundamental shift in thinking that has made all the difference.

Previously, Michael served as an assistant principal in Prosser, Washington, where he was named the 2010–2011 Three Rivers Principal Association Assistant Principal of the Year. In 2011–2012, Michael was a finalist for Washington Assistant Principal of the Year.

Michael earned his bachelor's degree in elementary education from Washington State University and his master's degree in educational leadership from Azusa Pacific University.

To learn more about Michael's work, visit https://everykidnow.com, or follow him @everykidnow on Twitter or Instagram.

To book Michael Roberts for professional development, contact pd@Solution Tree.com.

Introduction

"But how do *we* do it?"

This is always the question when a district or school is striving to become a professional learning community (PLC). Teachers and school leaders study books on the PLC process, learn from experts at conferences, and visit model PLC schools to see the work in action. But applying PLC practices to their own schools is often a hurdle. Even after thinking, learning, and researching, educators may still find themselves wondering, "How do *we* get a motivated group of teacher leaders to guide peers toward accomplishing the fundamental purpose of the school? How do *we* get staff to share best practices across campuses? How do *we* get all adults on campus and external stakeholders to understand where we are going?" These types of questions can be paralyzing to an organization's ability to develop a collaborative, *we*-oriented culture that will help all students learn at high levels. Yet, an absence of effective answers to these questions can prevent staff from even buying in to the idea of the collaborative process.

This book will guide you in responding to these questions, and it will do so by serving as a tool for you to use to confront the challenges that make these questions so daunting. Challenges include getting building administrators and teachers to see beyond their immediate *me* and look to a greater *we*, where best practices will support the learning of all students. When the entire school or district shares best practices, all students benefit. Yet many well-meaning, hardworking educators see it as a badge of honor to say things like, "I'm just worried about my students," or "My students are different." This single-mindedness is the paradigm most educators were raised in and has been a quality of great principals and teachers for over 130 years. Resetting individual thinking to a more global view of the district or school will take some work.

For example, I once had dinner with a lifelong friend who is a good teacher and a caring educator whom parents are excited to see on their students' schedules. When he heard I was supporting the development of professional learning communities, he grunted. He told me that one of his colleagues had been assigned to teach two sections of Advanced Placement U.S. history—his favorite class to teach. He went on to say he was frustrated because he had "built the program" and he was not happy that they were "both supposed to teach the same way." He wanted to just be left alone to teach.

The interesting thing is, he once told me that he became a better football coach the day he started sharing responsibility with his assistant coaches. When they shared more ideas on the offense, the team got more wins. In short, he became a better coach when he began collaborating. I pointed this out to him, but I do not think he heard the logic of my point. Changing his mind—and the minds of thousands like him who still believe their classrooms are their singular domains—will take a lot of work by district and building administrators and strong teacher leaders.

Another of these challenges is the need to customize the development and operation of a PLC to each individual school. While customization is a challenge, it is also an opportunity that allows—indeed requires—district administrators, building principals, and teacher leaders to think about and experiment with content so they can make connections and utilize their learning and resources to tailor the PLC process for their own schools. With the guidance of this book, educators will take on this opportunity, this work of thought and experimentation. They will learn to create customized tight-loose cultures (DuFour, DuFour, Eaker, Many, & Mattos, 2016), and in this process discover their non-negotiables to which all staff members will be accountable (the elements that are tight) while understanding in what ways collaborative teams and teachers may retain autonomy (the loose elements) to use their own professionalism and experience to determine the path they will take to meet the non-negotiable expectations.

After finishing this book, a district or school will have a process to follow. They will use their newly created systems and cultures to engender high levels of learning for all students and all staff. Teachers along with school and district leaders can use the process in this book in conjunction with the expert guidance of a PLC conference or professional development event, but these guidelines are equally useful for schools and districts embarking on a self-guided PLC journey. By sharing advice, common mistakes, and lessons learned, this book seeks to speed your district or school on its individual path toward becoming a true professional learning community. In the words of Kristopher Treat, a history teacher at Eastmark High School in Queen Creek, Arizona, becoming an accountable professional learning community "is not something you do wrong, wrong, wrong, perfect. It is a journey" (personal communication, June 3, 2018). An accountable professional learning community is when educators work collaboratively to urgently eliminate gaps that prevent students from learning grade-level content and systematically provide additional, meaningful learning for students when they demonstrate proficiency. Teams should keep that destination in mind, but note that while a district or school is on that journey, *we are trying* and *not yet* are legitimate answers to questions about progress.

"Can a district or school guarantee that all students, regardless of the teacher they have, will learn at high levels?"

"Not yet."

"Do all students get all the support they need to fill any gaps they may have in essential learning?"

"We are trying."

"Are proficient students extending their learning?"

"We are working on it."

Good—keep working, and hopefully this book will help guide you further down that road to becoming a true professional learning community.

To make this book easy to use, common questions for developing professional learning communities serve as the basis for each chapter. Each chapter addresses a question that school leaders often hear as they guide their schools toward becoming an accountable PLC. These questions come from all sides—teachers, parents, and community stakeholders. These questions were all posed directly to me when I was a building principal or district administrator, or to administrators I was working with. The chapters will provide specific information in response to the broad questions, followed by actionable steps to move an organization closer to becoming an accountable PLC.

Chapter 1 addresses the all-too-common issue of a school that conducts collaborative meetings, but the meetings have not had any effect on classroom instruction. In such a school, there is a disconnect between what is going on during collaborative time and the professional practices within the classroom. The investment of time is not leading to any kind of instructional payoff. The school is caught in what Richard DuFour and Douglas Reeves (2016) refer to as *PLC lite*. By focusing on how to clarify a school's mission and vision, this chapter will help you operate with purpose and start or restart down the road to becoming a true PLC.

Chapter 2 focuses on leading by example and on how to be a collaborative leader. Leaders will find guidance on how to select teacher leaders and remove obstacles by empowering these staff members.

Chapter 3 highlights the importance of a narrow set of collective commitments involving a district's or school's focus on student learning and key adult behaviors. This chapter discusses a process by which all staff share collective commitments, planning vital learning outcomes to ensure all students are learning at grade level or higher.

Chapter 4 focuses on instructional leadership. Getting leaders in the classrooms and out of offices more often is key to improving learning across the school or district. This chapter discusses the rationale for increasing time in classrooms and offers a template to make this happen. Leaders will find ideas for changing routine staff meetings and creating time for staff to observe one another with the aim of spreading best practices across the school. Finally, this chapter addresses inclusivity in school leadership. Every adult in the organization must be part of the mission of the school.

Chapter 5 helps leaders maintain a district's or school's focus when outside forces threaten to distract. Districts and schools must limit the number of initiatives and sustain these practices over multiple years to ensure success. The three big ideas and four critical questions of the PLC process are the perfect conduit for finding sustained focus (DuFour et al., 2016).

Chapter 6 underscores the importance of setting goals and celebrating progress. This chapter focuses on how to set effective goals, as well as when, why, and how to celebrate. Goals provide a road map and celebrations support hardworking staff members. By including students in celebrations, leaders can also acknowledge the daily hard work of the students who make up the district or school.

Chapter 7 will bring attention to how to inform parents and community stakeholders about what a professional learning community is and how it helps students learn more effectively. District, school, and teacher leaders will find suggestions for how to share this information with their governing board and parents in support of the mission, vision, and collective commitments.

At the beginning of each chapter, you will find a learning target that sets the intention for your reading. In the book *Classroom Assessment for Student Learning: Doing it Right—Using It Well,* Richard Stiggins, Judith Arter, Jan Chappuis, and Stephen Chappuis (2004) assert that "understanding the important learning targets is the essential foundation of sound assessment, and of good teaching too" (p. 15). This applies to adult educators seeking to expand their knowledge as much as it does students in the classroom. Two or three success criteria follow each chapter's learning target, which you may use to evaluate your own learning. As John Hattie (2009) states in *Visible Learning*:

> It helps if these learning intentions and success criteria are shared with, committed to, and understood by the learner—because in the right caring and idea-rich environment, the learner can experiment (be right or wrong) with the content and the thinking about the content, and make connections across ideas. (p. 23)

Each chapter also includes examples from real schools and comments from teachers who have worked through the transformation from PLC lite to accountable professional learning community. They provide insight into how making this fundamental shift improves teachers' jobs and students' experiences. Keep in mind that the examples you'll encounter are specific to the schools and staffs that arrived at these steps and collective commitments. Use them to increase your understanding and inspire *your* work while recognizing that your district or school must come up with its own systems. Do not simply copy what other sites have done, for there is no faster way to lose your way as an organization than to try and walk in another's footprints. Create your own path to high levels of learning for all students based on your organization's strengths and needs.

Finally, each chapter concludes with discussion questions and other practical resources to help you and your team enact and customize the concepts presented in the chapter. These resources serve as jumping-off points so leaders can create unique plans for helping their organizations become accountable PLCs. For it is these unique plans, developed within the framework of a professional learning community, that catalyze staff to move beyond the *me* culture that has not enabled all students to be successful and get them to begin working as a *we* and supporting all students to learn at grade level or better.

"We've Met for Years, so Why Hasn't It Changed My Practice?"

*The primary challenge in the PLC process is changing,
and not merely tweaking, the existing culture.*

—Richard DuFour

This chapter will cover the basics of establishing purpose and focus in a PLC. Staff members in schools where some collaborative elements are in place might resist PLC implementation by asking, "We've met for years, so why hasn't it changed my practice?" They think, "We've tried that already and it hasn't done any good." These sentiments reinforce the *me* culture that presumes one teacher working in isolation can get the same results as a group of teachers working together, but with a lot fewer headaches. Often teachers who think this way work in schools that exemplify PLC lite; avoiding this anemic version of the process is the first topic of this chapter. With that understanding as a foundation, readers will learn key factors for leading the journey to building a meaningful *we* culture and becoming an accountable PLC, as well as a process for establishing an organizational mission and vision.

Learning Target

My job after reading this chapter is to be able to lead my organization to establish a memorable mission and vision that will focus the transformation from PLC lite to an accountable professional learning community.

Success Criteria

▶ I know I have done my job if I can explain PLC lite and why it will not achieve the kind of results that will support all students learning at high levels.

▶ I know I have done my job if I can apply key business concepts (such as Lewin's [1947] change model and Heath and Heath's [2008] SUCCESs) to lead positive change in my organization.

▶ I know I have done my job if I can lead a manageable meeting that results in a clear mission and vision for my school or district.

Understanding PLC Lite

Since the 1998 publication of Richard DuFour and Robert Eaker's book *Professional Learning Communities at Work*®, the ideas and basic concepts of a PLC have spread throughout the education world. Most schools have heard of *the three big ideas* and *four critical questions* of a professional learning community and a lot of schools at least pay lip service to them. For clarity's sake, the three big ideas as put forth by DuFour and his colleagues (2016) in *Learning by Doing* are as follows.

1. **A focus on learning:** DuFour and colleagues (2016) explain, "The fundamental purpose of the school is to ensure that all students learn at high levels" (p. 11; with *high levels* being defined as grade level or higher).

2. **A collaborative culture and collective responsibility:** DuFour and colleagues (2016) assert, "Educators must work collaboratively and take collective responsibility for the success of each student" (p. 11).

3. **A results orientation:** Successful PLCs require a results orientation. DuFour and colleagues (2016) maintain, "To assess their effectiveness in helping all students learn, educators in a PLC focus on results— evidence of student learning" (p. 12).

The four critical questions of PLCs at Work are:

1. What is it we want our students to know and be able to do?
2. How will we know if each student has learned it?
3. How will we respond when some students do not learn it?
4. How will we extend the learning for students who have demonstrated proficiency? (DuFour et al., 2016, p. 59)

Unfortunately, as they spread, these ideas also became diluted in some cases and PLC lite runs rampant. DuFour and Reeves (2016) offer this definition of PLC lite:

> Educators rename their traditional faculty or department meetings as PLC meetings, engage in book studies that result in no action, or devote collaborative time to topics that have no effect on student achievement—all in the name of the PLC process. These activities fail to embrace the central tenets of the PLC process and won't lead to higher levels of learning for students or adults. (p. 69)

For school staff to say they adhere to PLC principles is one thing; to do the work is something else entirely.

Many teachers who work in PLC-lite schools may think some variation of "we've met for years, but it has never changed my practice." A few might even say this out loud. PLC-lite schools treat teachers' most finite resource—time—as though there is a huge surplus of it. PLC-lite schools mandate book studies that take months, with no expectation that the content of the book will change instruction in the classroom. PLC-lite schools put a group of teachers in a room together with little direction and less support and tell them to collaborate, which often results in frustration for the teachers and for the administrators who believed that just getting the teachers in the same room is enough. Schools practicing PLC lite engage in long debates and discussions of practices that have little or no effect on student learning. Hattie (2009) has identified both impactful and ineffectual practices in his extensive research, a synthesis of over 1,600 meta-analyses involving over three million students worldwide. For example, time spent discussing homework, different types of testing, or student retention may be wasted as Hattie's research shows these practices have only small positive effects or even negative effects on student learning during the school year.

PLC-lite schools are stuck in what DuFour (2014) describes as "convenient parking places" along the road to becoming a professional learning community. The organization has begun to make changes, but has not fully committed to becoming a professional learning community. When the adults become uncomfortable with the process, the district or school stops trying to get better. After all, they are better than they were. For example, perhaps a school guided teams of teachers to align their major units to be taught at the same time, but is unwilling to push the adults to identify essential standards, create team SMART goals, write common formative assessments, and collaborate around student data. In this scenario, the school has conveniently parked at coordinating units and is unwilling to advance the process further. Getting out of these parking spaces often requires an almost complete reset of the process. To get a district or site out of these metaphorical parking places, a leader should go back to why PLCs are a good idea in the first place and what it takes to make and keep commitments.

Consider the journey of Desert View Elementary School (DVES) in Hermiston, Oregon. This school community was initially stuck in PLC lite. This started to change one day when the leadership team announced a narrowed focus for the upcoming year. The community would direct its attention to just two focus areas: the first, improving initial classroom instruction; the second, learning how to collaborate and set aside time for meaningful collaboration. It was then that one of the teachers uttered the statement that thousands of teachers have probably thought about collaborative meetings over the years: "We've met for years, but it has never once changed my practice." I remember this statement very clearly, because I had just become principal at DVES.

This statement is definitive. It is black and white. There is finality to it. This feeling, that meetings that were supposed to make teaching an easier job are largely unproductive, is a common one. Thousands of teachers who would do anything necessary to ensure all the students in their classes become better students and better people find little or no value in meeting with their peers. Perhaps DVES leadership should have seen the concern and dismay coming. Some of them had attended a PLC conference three years prior. When they returned to school, they passed on the district message to begin "being a PLC" with little training or understanding for those who did not attend the conference. It was this lack of understanding of the process and reasons behind the process that led to many staff members feeling as though collaborative meetings were a waste of time. Others felt it was up to them as individuals to carry the weight of ineffective teachers through the collaborative process. It was in this context that the teacher made the "it's never changed what I do" comment. However, once concern is out in the open, district and school leaders can work on addressing it. Leaders need to make a commitment themselves and ensure the time teachers invest in discussing their practice and digging into student data will generate benefits in the form of higher student achievement.

DVES was stuck in PLC lite, with a low opinion of collaboration and many divisions among the staff. One of the divisions stemmed from the differences between how teachers viewed themselves versus their colleagues. Figures 1.1 and 1.2 display the results of the two following staff survey questions.

1. How often are you willing to work at changing DVES for the better? How often are your colleagues willing to work at changing DVES for the better?

2. How often do you welcome new and innovative ideas? How often do your colleagues welcome new and innovative ideas?

The survey clearly shows that individuals thought they were willing to do more themselves than their colleagues were willing to do. This perception led to staff members feeling their work was unappreciated and that they were bearing more than their share of responsibility for work meant to benefit the whole community. Long story short, in spite of staff being placed in groups for years, a lot of work needed to be done to create a cohesive learning community at this school—one that everyone felt committed to.

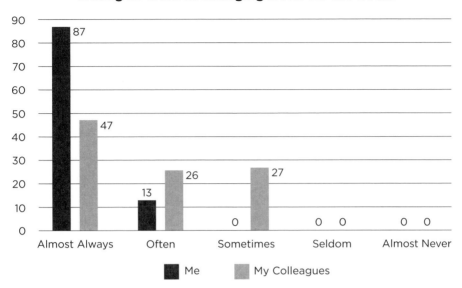

Source: © 2013 by Hermiston School District. Used with permission.

Figure 1.1: Perceptions of willingness to work at improving DVES.

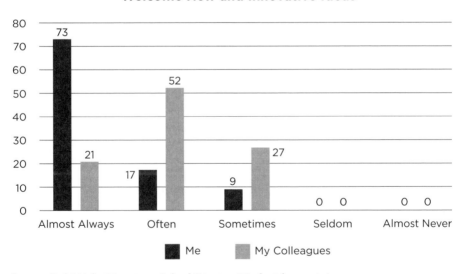

Source: © 2013 by Hermiston School District. Used with permission.

Figure 1.2: Perceptions of openness to new and innovative ideas.

When the leadership team received the survey results, the leaders were not particularly surprised. As with a lot of districts or schools, a few people had attended an inspiring institute or summit and returned to the site fired up and ready to help all students learn. At the conference, speakers had expounded on the power of collaboration and what it can do for the adults and students. The attendees returned home and placed people in teams and waited for the magic to happen. What was left out was a meaningful plan for engagement along with steps to do so. DuFour and colleagues (2016) affirm the importance of taking steps to ensure collaboration.

> Simply organizing people into teams does not improve a school. Steps must be taken to ensure that those teams engage in collaboration on the issues that most impact student learning. (p. 75)

At DVES, the leadership team set about rectifying this lack of understanding and follow-through by planning how to focus on "issues that most impact student learning" (DuFour et al., 2016, p. 75). Fortunately for the hundreds of students who attended Desert View, this set the school on a path from a good school to a model PLC school and eventually to DuFour Award runner-up. In addition to its tremendous growth over the next four years (Oregon Department of Education [ODE] Quality Education Commission, 2018), DVES was recognized as one of six schools in Oregon with diverse populations (over 30 percent students of color) that performed in the top 5 percent of the state academically (ODE Quality Education Commission, 2018).

Leading the Journey to Accountability

To avoid falling into the trap of PLC lite and to guide their schools and districts along the road to success, leaders need to understand and enact several key factors. The following sections discuss the importance of these factors, which include developing productive identities, utilizing the unfreeze-change-refreeze model for leading an organization's transformation, and ensuring key ideas persist over time to become part of an organization's culture.

Personal and Organizational Identities

As the title of this book suggests, building a collaborative, *we*-oriented culture is an essential part of becoming an accountable PLC. Traditionally, teaching is an individual and sometimes isolated profession, with teachers confined to their own classrooms, doing things their own way. Teachers who are accustomed to that culture may have very strong personal identities and fear losing these identities to the collective. On occasion, a teacher will resist an organization's move toward becoming a PLC because he or she has an established reputation. Perhaps the teacher has received accolades for being the best third-grade teacher or is known as the one who teaches all the AP calculus classes. Even such a high-quality educator may resist committing to meaningful collaboration and thinking about all students (not just those in his or her class) if he or she fears losing part of his or her identity.

Imagine an expert teacher who is known throughout his school as *the math guru*. His colleagues refer to him as the math guru; perhaps even his principal uses this term. All the other teachers know that he is the best math teacher and his students achieve great results. This is his personal identity, and it has taken him the better part of two decades to build it. It's very possible that such a teacher would be resistant to the changing culture. His reticence to share responsibility to ensure all students learn might involve a fear of losing his math-guru identity if his students do not outscore every other class across the district.

Fear of identity loss is a very real and common concern that the administrator must handle deftly to move the school along in the collaborative process. To support a staff member through this delicate process, one must understand that change will be difficult for a person who has done a great deal of thinking about identity and explored what it took to reach this place in life (Anthis, 2013). To counteract this, the leader can speak about a vision of possible new identities. For example, to get the math guru to embrace change, the principal could work with him so he comes to see himself as a leader of the collaborative process. To do this, the principal could ask him to vet professional learning before it is presented to the rest of the staff or invite him to give recommendations for how to train staff. By asking this staff member to give input on articles to read, videos to view, or training activities, the leader redirects his thinking from *me* (his classroom, his practice) to *we* (our training, our school). As this process continues, he will begin developing a new work identity. In this case, teacher-learning guru will replace math guru.

In a 2017 study of over 2,900 teachers in Sweden, researchers Ola Nordhall and Igor Knez found that teachers' personal identities at work are largely emotionally based, while organizational identity is more cognitively based. When a teacher is clinging to the idea that he or she is the subject guru or the best teacher of a certain grade, the learning leader needs to make sure to provide enough sound information and data that the cognitive part of the brain bypasses the emotional part (Nordhall & Knez, 2018). Only then will the teacher be willing to consider addressing grade-, school-, or district-level matters as a *we* rather than as the *me* of his or her individual classroom.

A Model for Transformation

In order to lead the transition from PLC lite to operating as a true PLC, it is helpful to have a model for conceptualizing the change process. One such model was developed by Kurt Lewin, an early 20th century psychologist. Lewin referred to his model as the *unfreeze-change-refreeze* model. This model has three distinct phases (Hattangadi, 2016; Lewin, 1947).

1. **Unfreeze:** Organizations realize change needs to happen and those within the organization feel the urgency for change and weigh the benefits versus possible damages. When the benefits outweigh possible damage, the organization begins to move.

2. **Change:** The members of the organization make the inner shifts required to accommodate the change. The next piece of the transition phase is when adjustments to the new system are made to support the strengths and weaknesses of those within the organization.

3. **Refreeze:** The change has been made, a new status quo has been achieved, and the accepted change is the new norm.

Using this model, the leader of a PLC-lite school needs to unfreeze the staff and culture to begin the change process. Consider the following three steps.

1. Redefine what a professional learning community is and how regular collaboration can support teachers' work.

2. Build an urgency around why this work is so very important to all student learning.

3. Reassure the staff that their individual art of teaching will not be lost in the process.

The leader then needs to support the staff through the change phase with the following four steps and recognitions.

1. Recognize change is difficult and takes time.

2. Support staff with professional learning so they can envision what true collaboration looks like.

3. Limit the number of initiatives staff are asked to learn and execute.

4. Celebrate the change as it is happening.

Once through the change phase, the leader needs to refreeze the new system with the following three actions.

1. Sustain the development of the school as a professional learning community over multiple years.

2. Align all new initiatives with the PLC process. Continually ask, "How does this look in a PLC? How does it fit with the three big ideas and four essential questions of a PLC?"

3. Celebrate the difficult changes staff have made to their practices. As the change process continues, what is celebrated will be remembered.

Ideas That Stick

Recognition of the need for change and familiarity with the model for change are a start, but leaders must ensure that change is permanent. The core tenets of professional learning communities certainly need to endure if a school is to operate as a successful PLC, as do the specific features of an individual school's systems and culture. Making sure new concepts stick is also critical to the refreeze stage of the change process. As such, leaders can construct and convey ideas in memorable, durable ways.

Chip Heath and Dan Heath's (2008) book *Made to Stick* examines why some ideas stay with an organization over time and become part of the culture while others fade. They sum up their findings with the acronym *SUCCESs*. According to Heath and Heath (2008), ideas that persist are **S**imple, **U**nexpected, **C**oncrete, **C**redible, **E**motional, and conveyed in **S**tories.

- **Simple:** Ideas that stick are easy for the group to understand and later retell. People quickly forget ideas that are overly complex in theory or language. One needs simply to think of phrases that become part of popular culture (for example, "Just Do It," "I'm Lovin' It," or "Got Milk?") to see the power of a simple message. Leaders looking to incorporate a simple message could ask, "Can this fit on a T-shirt?" Simple ideas like "all students will learn" or "every student, every day" can communicate everything a leader wants his or her organization to be. One word of caution: to make these simple ideas resonate, teams within the organization must do the work to reinforce these simple ideas. Without the research-based activities to guarantee all students will learn, these ideas will only be slogans and not the central idea that drives an organization.

- **Unexpected:** An unexpected twist can make new ideas memorable to a large group of people. As one example, the movie *The Empire Strikes Back* (part of the *Star Wars* series; Kurtz & Kershner, 1980) achieved its place in popular culture not because of any spaceship battle, but for the unexpected revelation that Darth Vader is Luke Skywalker's father. For educational leaders, finding an expected twist that resonates with the organization can lead more people to remember and retell the story.

- **Concrete:** Concrete ideas resonate with people. Ideas that staff members can understand and act on work better than abstract concepts. Educational leaders can turn to educational research to support ideas with concrete evidence. When an organization is beginning the transition to becoming a PLC, leaders can turn to the book *Learning by Doing* (DuFour et al., 2016) to guide the staff's professional learning. This concrete resource will allow teachers to put their hands on the processes of a PLC and the research behind those processes.

- **Credible:** People are much more likely to adopt an idea if it is believable and well supported. Is the idea credible? Is there research behind it? Can it be done within the given organizational constraints? Does the person delivering the message have credibility? All of these questions need to be answered in the affirmative in order for an idea to be credible. If a respected researcher or expert delivers a message, it will carry more weight than if a newly hired principal or superintendent delivers the same message.

- **Emotional:** Connecting to an individual's emotions will help imprint an idea in the person's memory and stir conversations weeks after the message is first delivered. This concept is essential in advertising. In the 1980s, for example, long-distance telephone companies played on emotions with ads featuring a grandfather reading a story to a toddler over the phone or a mother receiving a call from her son stationed overseas. To help an idea resonate within a district or school, the leader can help educators draw on their emotional connections with their students. Leaders should draw a clear link between this new information and supporting specific current or former students that teachers care about.

- **Stories:** Stories resonate. This resonance is why people recount movies to friends or retell jokes. If a leader wants an idea to become part of the culture of an organization, tying it to a memorable story is one of the best ways to ensure this happens. Any district or school contains literally hundreds of stories. A leader can pick a current or former student's story to illustrate the need for the organization to ensure all students are learning or why becoming a PLC will make a difference for the student.

When all of these elements are in place, members of the district or school can easily remember and communicate the ideas that need to become part of the culture of the school.

When enacting the SUCCESs acronym in terms of building a professional learning community, a leader should start with the school's mission and vision. Making the mission and vision concrete and simple is a key part of the unfreezing stage. Doing so will go a long way toward redefining what a PLC is and how it can support high levels of learning for all students while creating urgency to support that learning.

Establishing Your Mission and Vision

Simon Sinek (2009; TEDx Talks, 2009), in his TED talk and book both titled *Start With Why*, maintains that without a clear *why* an organization will struggle to complete any initiative. DuFour, DuFour, Eaker, and Karhanek (2004) agree with Sinek and take the point further in *Whatever It Takes: How Professional Learning Communities Respond When Kids Don't Learn*. Only the learning leader of an organization can engrain the *why* in a district's or school's operation: "Principals who hope to lead learning communities must be unequivocal champions, promoters, and protectors of key PLC concepts, and that is not a job they can delegate to someone else" (p. 147). The same responsibility may rest with the district administrator. It is the person in charge of the organization who must make sure that the organization is bypassing those convenient parking places that DuFour (2014) warned about and continuing down a road that can be difficult to travel.

Each student becoming successful and learning at high levels is a central mission of all schools. It is the compelling purpose that explains the organization's existence and the driving force behind all improvement efforts. Students learning is the mission of every educational entity. Students being prepared for whatever comes next in life is the vision all caring, hardworking educators have for their students. Districts and schools do not need to make it more complicated than that.

Does your school or district have a mission and vision already? Just because there is a saying on the letterhead or on the home page of the website does not mean that an organization truly has a mission and vision. I once visited a school where the mission statement was painted on the wall in the main hallway, on a mural seven feet high and sixteen feet long. No one entering the building could miss it, but when I asked the staff to recite the mission, they gave me befuddled looks. Not one staff member even got close. When I read the mission statement from the pictures I had taken (it was too big to fit in one picture), the staff let out a collective *ahh*. One teacher explained that the statement had been painted a decade earlier, when the school was built. The school's mission had been rewritten since then, so no one paid attention to the mural anymore. The wall had not been repainted (and, by the way, nobody knew the new mission statement either).

To test your mission and vision, you can conduct a similar exercise. At the next leadership meeting or staff meeting, ask those present to recite the mission or vision statement from memory. You might make it interesting by offering a prize like a coffee gift card or a ream of extra copy paper. Can anyone recite the mission or vision statements that a committee spent hours putting together and wordsmithing? If not, then the organization does not have a mission or a vision. Instead, the organization has a string of words that does not mean much. This is an all-too-common issue in schools. At some point, a committee of people wrote a mission statement that is too long, infused with flowery language, devoid of clear meaning, and quickly forgotten.

Another way to check the quality of an organization's mission or vision statement is for the district's or school's guiding coalition or leadership team to play mission and vision bingo. A bingo card is provided in figure 1.3. First, to better understand why flowery language and vague buzzwords are not helpful, the guiding coalition should look at the bingo card and try to concretely describe what the terms look like at the classroom level. Some of the phrases will be difficult to apply to a first-grade class or an Advanced Placement chemistry course, for example, because they lack practical meaning in school contexts.

Next, the superintendent or principal would have someone on the team pull up a copy of the current mission statement for the district or school. Then compare the bingo card to the mission statement. If a district's or school's mission or vision statement can produce a bingo—or worse, a blackout—on the card then the statement is probably too long and contains too much flowery language to have a clear, actionable meaning at the classroom level.

In *Starting a Movement*, Ken Williams and Tom Hierck (2015) state that "becoming your ideal school begins with examining your culture, fundamental purpose, and commitment to ensuring learning for all" (p. 8). Clear, concise, and meaningful mission and vision statements should unambiguously speak to what the leadership and teachers envision for the students who attend their district or school. Proper mission and vision statements drive the organization's actions and are not just written down for the sake of writing them down. If nobody knows a district's or school's mission and vision statements, then, on any practical level, the mission statement does not exist. Being mission- and vision-driven means all staff understand the *why* of the

B	I	N	G	O
21st Century	Critical Thinkers	Responsible	Diverse or Diversity	Engages or Engagement
Feel Valued	Collaboration	Social-Emotional	Nurture	Lifetime Learner
Citizens	High Expectations	**Free Space**	Welcoming	Positive
Excellence	Problem Solvers	Respect or Respectful	Self-Directed	Natural Abilities
Growth Mindset	Inspire	Cultivate	Empower	Rigor

Figure 1.3: Mission and vision bingo.

organization and are willing to actively support that purpose—or at the very least not work against it.

In *Learning by Doing*, DuFour and colleagues (2016) assert that mission statements define the reason schools exist, while vision statements speak to a compelling future. For example, a clear mission statement might be "Preparing all students for the future." Then, a clear vision statement illustrates how the high ideals of the mission statement will come to fruition. A vision statement that corresponds to the previous mission could be "engaging all learners through quality teaching, collaboration, and relationships." This clearly lays out for all stakeholders that they will achieve their mission by employing three areas of focus: quality teaching, collaboration, and building relationships. There is no confusion as to what the faculty will do to support their students.

The key to writing concise, useful missions and visions, in the words of Robert Eaker and Janel Keating (2012), is to do so "without wallowing in the work" (p. 28)—that is to say, without spending an inordinate amount of time on something that should be done fairly quickly. The longer it takes to write mission and vision statements, the more they tend to grow in length and complexity and the less likely it is that staff, students, and parents will be able to remember them. Instead, districts and schools should follow two key elements of the SUCCESs model (Heath & Heath, 2008) and make the mission and vision statements simple and concrete. Mission statements like "Every student ready for the future," "Educating all students," or "Improving every student's life through education" are easy to remember and free of flowery, confusing language. Please note that leaders must not confuse writing mission and vision statements with living one's mission (DuFour et al., 2016). Once an organization has written its simple, concrete mission and vision statements, it needs to allocate resources to support the mission and vision.

Guidelines for developing a mission and vision in a forty-five-minute staff meeting appear at the end of this chapter (page 25). By following these steps, the leader can begin to ease the organization into a renewed purpose with re-established mission and vision statements that lead to collective commitments that the staff are willing and able to carry out. Including staff in the creation of the mission and vision and getting their approval helps establish credibility, the second C in the SUCCESs model (Heath & Heath, 2008).

Once the staff have crafted a simple and concrete mission and vision, leaders should share them publicly along with the collective commitments. These collective commitments will lay out how the compelling future will be accomplished (DuFour et al., 2016). We will further discuss collective commitments in chapter 3 (page 43). As a leader attempts to refreeze the

 TEACHER PERSPECTIVE

Garth Lind taught high school mathematics before moving to the upper-elementary level. He said that common mission, vision, and commitments really helped his school in becoming an accountable PLC. These elements eliminated misconceptions about the collaborative process. His team planned and graded everything together. But, one of the biggest changes that came with collaboration was the ability to say, "I don't know." Every team member felt free to say, "I don't know" and then the team would figure out the issue together. This was easy for the team because teachers used the same lesson plans and exemplars, and they all had the same expectations, which aligned with the vision of the school (G. Lind, personal communication, June 29, 2019).

mission and vision into the district's or school's culture, unexpected and emotional stories (the remaining elements of the SUCCESs framework) will be an important tool. Every classroom in every school contains unexpected, emotional stories, and these stories are compelling reasons why a district or school must commit to all students learning at grade level or higher. To focus staff on these unexpected, emotional stories, the learning leader can ask the staff to identify students they have worked with in the past who rose above their circumstances to learn at a high level. When given this direction, educators often share stories of students who were homeless, lost a parent or sibling, or came from generations of poverty, yet were successful in school.

Summary

In an environment where PLC lite (DuFour & Reeves, 2016) has been the accepted model for years, a leader must return to the work of Heath and Heath (2008), Lewin (1947), and Sinek (2009; TEDx Talks, 2009). By re-establishing the research behind why the PLC process is the best way to support every student, the leader is unfreezing the staff by establishing a clear purpose for the school's daily work—*every student learning at high levels*. The mission and vision need to be simple, concrete, credible, and tied into the unexpected, emotional stories of the students these caring adults serve.

Chapter 1 Discussion Questions

1. Is our district or school engaged in PLC-lite activities? Or are we on the road to being an accountable professional learning community?

2. Would an anonymous survey of the staff benefit our work? What should we ask? How and when will we share the results with the staff?

3. Which business concept resonates with you the most? How will that concept be applied to lead organizational change?

4. I predict that _____ percent of staff can recite our mission and vision statements. Why do staff remember or fail to remember our mission and vision statements?

5. In what ways will the organization struggle with the forty-five-minute mission and vision meeting? What parts should go well? When can we schedule the meeting?

Chapter 1 Reflection Worksheet

Learning Target

My job after reading this chapter is to be able to lead my organization to establish a memorable mission and vision that will focus the transformation from PLC lite to accountable professional learning community.

Success Criteria

▸ *I know I have done my job if I can explain PLC lite and why it will not achieve the kind of results that will support all students learning at high levels.*

▸ *I know I have done my job if I can apply key business concepts (such as Lewin's change model and Heath and Heath's SUCCESs) to lead positive change in my organization.*

▸ *I know I have done my job if I can lead a manageable meeting that results in a clear mission and vision for my school or district.*

I would restate the learning target for this chapter in this way:

If I had to pick one idea or concept from this chapter that really stands out, it would be:

The concept or idea that sparks my imagination is:

Those imaginative ideas are:

The success criterion that gives me the biggest challenge is:

Steps I can take to help overcome that challenge are:

Mission and Vision in Forty-Five Minutes

1. Gather all staff members and clearly establish the target and criteria for success for the next forty-five minutes.

   › *Example target*—At the end of the meeting, we will have mission and vision statements that everyone can support and carry out.

   › *Example success criteria*—Everyone can remember and recite the agreed-on mission and vision statements.

   For clarity's sake, the agreed-on mission and vision statements will be as free from educational jargon as possible.

   Going forward, all interactions with students and stakeholders will reflect the agreed-on mission and vision statements.

2. Place staff in groups cutting across departments, grade levels, and job categories. Doing this breaks up cliques and establishes a whole-district or whole-school understanding of the work. After choosing groups, the leader should pay special attention to balance the groups. Staff members who may be negative should be placed in groups with a staff member who will be positive. Staff who tend to dominate conversations should be in a group with staff members who tend to ensure all voices are heard. Balance is the key word for these groups. The groups will start their work with the mission statement.

3. Once settled, staff get sixty seconds to write down a disposition they would like for their child, grandchild, niece, or nephew to have when that child is done with high school. If a staff member does not have any of these connections, he or she can picture a former student. For example, staff may write down *happy*, *ready for the world*, *capable*, or *able to do whatever they desire*. The key is for the disposition to be short, free of excessive commas, and meaningful.

4. Teams share the dispositions they have written and then vote on the their favorite one. If teams are really struggling with a couple of the dispositions they really like, a leader can allow them to share both. However, he or she must keep in mind the goal is to create something short, meaningful, and easily remembered.

5. The agreed-on dispositions are shared out to the room. The leader records the dispositions on note cards that are taped up or pinned to a wall for all to see. The recommendation to use note cards here is for ease of movement later in the process.

6. Staff then discuss if any of the dispositions can be combined with like ideas. A leader may have ten cards on the wall at the start of this process, but combining cards that say *follow their passion* with ones that read *do what they love* and *excited for life* can quickly reduce the number of cards.

7. When the cards are fewer, each staff member gets one vote. The vote mechanism can be a round colored sticker or a small star sticker. Staff are then invited to place their value vote on *one* card. The stickers are used for a concrete, visually obvious record that demonstrates the will of the group. One or two cards will emerge as clear favorites. If this is not the case following the first balloting, then the dispositions clearly not among the favorites can be eliminated and the voting can happen again. If there are two favorites—for example, one card has twenty-one votes another has eighteen and the remaining fifteen votes are dispersed across six cards—can the favorites be combined into one statement?

8. Use the favorite disposition to quickly write a draft mission statement. The leader should remember that the staff are creating a mission: the fundamental purpose for the organization. After participants create the rough-draft statement, the leader should ask if they can live with the statement. If everyone assents, the leader should tell the staff that the leadership team may wordsmith the disposition a little, but they are moving on to the vision statement. The key point here is to ask staff members if they *can live with* the proposed mission statement, not necessarily if they agree 100 percent with every variation of it. Asking for total agreement can lead to nitpicking of language, but general assent to a greater idea will keep the meeting moving forward without being distracted by the minutiae of semantics. Next, the leader will guide the groups on to creating the vision statement.

9. The leader poses the question, "What is one thing we need to do to make the mission statement we just agreed on come true?" The leader then goes back through the process, this time with staff focusing on what they need to do to bring their vision of a compelling

future for all students to fruition. Ideas come from the groups, the groups record them on the cards, they combine the cards, and staff vote on which ideas will instill in all students the vital disposition they agreed to. This time the leader may want to accept the top two or three ideas if the group can make them into a memorable statement. For example, if the top three cards say *collaborate, support students' emotional wellbeing*, and *high expectations*, the vision statement can be: *through collaboration, Mary Snitly Middle School will hold all students to high academic expectations while supporting their emotional wellbeing.* Although this statement dances dangerously close to bingo-card territory, by limiting the statement to three ideas, it becomes more memorable and therefore more meaningful. If a leader wants to steer entirely clear of complicated structure and language, the following statement covers the same ground in different language: *the staff at Mary Snitly Middle School will work together to ensure all students learn at high levels while feeling safe and loved.*

10. Share new mission and vision statements; review the meeting target and success criteria.

   › *Example new mission statement*—"Every student will leave Mary Snitly Middle School with the skills needed to do what he or she loves."

   › *Example new vision statement*—"The staff at Mary Snitly Middle School will work together to ensure all students learn at high levels while feeling safe and loved."

   › *Example target review*—At the end of the meeting, Mary Snitly Middle School will have mission and vision statements that everyone can support and carry out; did we accomplish that?

   › *Example success criteria review*—Can everyone remember and recite the agreed-on mission and vision statements? If so, do it now.

   Are the agreed-on mission and vision statements as free from educational jargon as possible?

   From this meeting forward can all interactions with students and stakeholders reflect the agreed-on mission and vision statements?

11. Thank everyone for coming and participating in the mission and vision meeting. Let everyone know the next step is creating collective commitments (see chapter 3, page 43) so they can all commit to making these statements come true.

12. After the meeting, the leader needs to share the new mission and vision for the school. Verbiage on the website may need to be changed, email signatures need to be adjusted, and so on.

"If We're Collaborating, Why Aren't You?"

Educators are a part of an intricate web, each contributing to the success or failure of their system.

—Anthony Muhammad and Luis Cruz

Much of the writing, thinking, and talking about professional learning communities focuses on the role of teachers and collaborative teams of teachers (DuFour et al., 2016). At a school level, staff are trained to think of all students and classrooms, not just their own. Leaders encourage teachers to embrace the process of working together to find solutions that support all students. Yet, when key decisions are made, it is often the leader, working in isolation, who makes them. The leader then expects teachers—or at the district level, school sites—to work collaboratively even though he or she didn't look outside his or her office for input on these key decisions. Thus, many teachers may wonder or ask their leaders, "If we're collaborating, why aren't you?"

A leader may ask him- or herself, "Wouldn't it be easier if I just decide and then train everyone to support my decision?" The short answer is *no*. Make no mistake, there are times

Learning Target

My job after reading this chapter is to collaborate with teacher colleagues to build an effective, focused guiding coalition.

Success Criteria

▶ I know I have done my job when I can explain some of the key research behind building a guiding coalition.

▶ I know I have done my job when I can explain to the guiding coalition why focusing on a few key initiatives is important and how it can affect the entire district or school.

▶ I know I have done my job when I can recognize key staff members who will lead others to commit to the PLC process.

when leaders need to make top-down decisions. At those times, either on a district or school level, a leader needs to be decisive. However, day-to-day leadership operations should be collaborative. A leader needs to be as collaborative as he or she expects teacher teams to be. Leading by example in this way is essential to shifting the school or district culture from the individual (me) to the collaborative (we).

Collaborative leadership work needs to begin with a guiding coalition of knowledgeable, well-respected, trusted staff members (DuFour et al., 2016) who can work with the leader to develop, vet, and roll out new initiatives. A community of professionals who access each other's experience and expertise will come up with better ideas. Collaboration results in decisions that everyone can live with, if not whole-heartedly support. The vision of a district or school collaborating at a high level to support all students learning does not stand a chance of being successful without key district and teacher leaders to support the work.

This chapter will establish the importance of collaborative leadership before covering how to form a guiding coalition and lead as a team. Please note that the terms *guiding coalition* and *leadership team* are used interchangeably. It does not matter what a school or district decides to call the group of professionals who set the direction of the organization and support and guide their peers. What is important is that such a team exists, and that it is made up of the right people (that is, people who give the group energy, balance, and diversity), and that their expertise is accessed regularly.

Collaborating for Leadership

Consider the following comparison between two schools I have worked with. These two different schools were in the same district with the same goal: to become a PLC where all students will have academic success. When I began working with the principals and the staffs, I discussed with both the same key steps and made the same recommendations.

On one campus, the principal formed a guiding coalition of teachers and empowered her teams to make decisions around which essential standards all students needed to master and how they would assess whether the students were being successful on those standards. She relied on her guiding coalition members to deliver professional learning and drive this work forward. When best practices were shared, it was the teachers who shared them. A synergy formed among staff and students. The collaborative work took off and student learning skyrocketed.

On the other campus, the principal formed a guiding coalition but then worked alone to set the agenda for the coalition meetings. The principal designed the professional learning for the staff. The principal tried to drive the collaborative process forward. It was not very long before the school became stuck in a PLC-lite quagmire. The meetings were seen as meaningless as most teams on campus filled the allotted time with busywork before returning to their classes to do the same old things. Teams created agendas and notes simply to appease the principal. Student learning did not improve, students' problem behaviors and disengagement continued, and adult drama surfaced regularly.

The biggest difference between these two schools was the learning leader guiding the process or controlling the process. A PLC has to be led by a leader who is willing to collaborate. The principal cannot insist the best thing for students is for the teachers to work together to solve problems if he or she is unwilling to do the same.

The messianic leader standing against all odds to create an educational paradise out of ashes does not exist. This is a myth. James Kouzes and Barry Posner (2010), in their book *The Truth About Leadership*, expose this fantasy when they state, "No leader ever got anything extraordinary done without the talent and support of others" (p. xxii). Sharon Kramer and Sarah Schuhl (2017) remind us:

> The most powerful and effective role the principal assumes is that of lead learner, not expert or "all-knowing one." Leadership that gets real results is collaborative; it's a process that involves building a school leadership team. (p. 8)

J. P. Kotter (2014) reminds leaders that an organization needs

> additional people with their own particular windows on the world and their additional good working relationships with others, in order to truly innovate. More people need to be able to have the latitude to initiate—not just carry out someone else's directives. (p. 23)

It is vital that the learning leader keeps in mind that teacher leaders cannot be an overlooked resource. In the examples at the beginning of this section, the solitary leader's actions led to apathy while the collaborative leader caused the teachers to feel ownership of the PLC process. It is this ownership that will lead to some of the most innovative and effective solutions.

In *The Collaborative Administrator*, Austin Buffum and his colleagues (2008) implore schools and districts to "create conditions in which both the depth and breadth of teacher leadership develop to become the very culture in which we conduct our day-to-day work" (p. 39). As teachers select essential standards, write SMART goals, and build common formative assessments, their ownership of the day-to-day work increases. This allows any teacher to emerge as a leader on any facet of the work, which builds the *we* culture that is required to become a professional learning community.

TEACHER PERSPECTIVE

Melissa Purswell, a middle school teacher and leadership team member, said that when her school made the shift to an accountable PLC from PLC lite, she finally understood what collaborative leadership could look like and how important the teachers were to the leadership of the school. Leadership team members helped plan professional development, including suggesting fellow teachers' best practices to serve as exemplars, celebrations, and recruiting teachers to join the staff. Ms. Purswell also noted that leadership team members had the freedom to challenge some of the policy decisions of the principal (M. Purswell, personal communication, November 30, 2019).

Anthony Muhammad (2018) also discusses the influence of collaborative leadership on culture in *Transforming School Culture*. He discusses two distinct cultures in every school: the formal and the informal. Muhammad states that the formal culture (the staff meeting, the conversations with the administrator) is by far much weaker than the informal culture (the parking lot conversation or Friday night at the local pub). Because administrators cannot be involved in the informal culture, it is vital that teacher leaders are active supporters of the direction of the school or district in the informal culture (Muhammad, 2018).

Luis Cruz is fond of saying that people do not tear down fences they helped build (L. Cruz, personal communication, August 24, 2014). By Cruz's reckoning, using the guiding coalition of staff members is vital, because having teachers help set the direction and key initiatives of a school will create a team of people willing and able to champion the vision of where the school is heading, especially during discussions within the informal culture (Muhammad, 2018).

Forming a Guiding Coalition

Because the guiding coalition is so important to the growth of a professional learning community and the establishment of the school's or district's goals, it should not be put together without deliberate thought. The staff must view the members of the guiding coalition as credible leaders. Guiding coalition members must be willing and able to articulate the goals of the district or school. Individuals who do not meet these conditions should not be part of the leadership team. Noncredible or inarticulate leaders can hinder the transition of an organization from PLC lite to accountable PLC. A tool to help leaders select guiding coalition members is provided later in the chapter (figure 2.1, page 35), but the leader should not discount his or her own conversations and experiences with district and school staff. Informal discussions with staff will regularly inform a leader which employees are well respected by their colleagues and who is excited to shift the school to a *we* culture and who would rather remain a *me*.

The members of the guiding coalition also need to be able to work together effectively. That is not to say that only staff who agree with the leader should be selected—far from it. Having team members who are willing to challenge the status quo or push the team to develop its ideas is important. Jon Gordon and Mike Smith (2015), in their book *You Win in the Locker Room First*, discuss the importance of leadership being willing and able to disagree in a productive, professional manner.

> We understood that you could not take anything personally in these meetings. We had to be willing to disagree in order to consider all possible plans and come up with the best one. It was uncomfortable at times because in our quest to get better there were always different views and strong opinions. (p. 146)

This same concept is important in developing productive collaborative teams. Teacher Kara Frazier identifies the willingness of team members to disagree with one another as a key component to building an accountable, interdependent collaborative team (K. Frazier, personal communication, April 17, 2019). There is value in professional practice that comes from teams discussing, disagreeing about, and then discussing again how a student's growth in reading should be measured, or in members having differing opinions about how best to help students understand graphing linear equations, for example. Some might say direct instruction is best, others guided practice or a kinesthetic activity followed by a collaborative assignment. Different perspectives, and willingness to navigate these different perspectives, are important.

On occasion, a leader will intentionally select a member of the guiding coalition who disagrees with the leader on the direction in which the organization should move. Before doing this, the leader needs to keep in mind that while this reluctant team member can bring valuable counterpoints and balance to the team, he or she may also sow discord in the team or among the staff. A leader should not have several of these reluctant team members on the guiding coalition at once, as one difficult person is manageable and valuable for his or her unique perspectives, but two or three such people can bring the important work of the team to a halt.

Whether it is a collaborative team or a guiding coalition, disagreement is a healthy, necessary part of moving a district, school, or team forward. AppFirst CEO David

TEACHER PERSPECTIVE

Rachel Lind was a long-time member of her school's leadership team. She noted there was a marked difference once her team committed to moving away from PLC lite to becoming an accountable professional learning community. Mrs. Lind said that learning how to truly collaborate instead of simply filling the meeting time gave the team a focus to help lead the school (R. Lind, personal communication, June 29, 2019).

Roth (2013) points out that dealing with team disagreement in a productive manner shows staff that all opinions matter. It also sets an expectation that everyone will support the ultimate decision because the team heard all sides during the process. When putting the guiding coalition together, the leader needs to consider team members who are willing to disagree without being obstructionist. Figure 2.1 is an example of a form that helps a leader consider individual team members for the guiding coalition as well as the make-up of the whole team to ensure the right balance and create a group that is able and willing to take on the important task of leading the district's or school's development. A blank reproducible version of the form appears at the end of this chapter (page 42).

Leading as a Team

Forming a guiding coalition with the right teacher leaders is only a start. Once a leader has selected team members to help lead the district or school, they need to do just that—lead. For a leader to assemble a great team and then use them merely to manage the day-to-day comings and goings of an organization is folly. This team needs to be fully engaged in discussions about staff professional learning and about how it affects student learning. Only then will an organization or site truly change.

The coalition's overarching task is to limit the number of initiatives that the district or school works on at one time. In *Cultures Built to Last*, Richard DuFour and Michael Fullan (2013) remind us of what effective teams do:

> Those who hope to lead systematic change must maintain a laser-like focus on a few key priorities, develop people throughout the organization to help lead the change, make adjustments as they learn from their successes and failures, and, very importantly, stay the course. (p. 29)

The principle of a tight focus on very few things over an extended period of time is a recurring theme for many schools that experience growth. For a school's journey from PLC lite to accountable PLC, the leadership team may choose as its focus

Possible Team Members	Subject or Grade Level	Assets		Liabilities
Watts	Mathematics	Well respected, students consistently highest achieving		Only been at the school for three years
Cook	Science	Thoughtful, well versed in many teaching styles		Can be standoffish
Harris	History	Well-liked and respected teacher		None
Sorrento	Language Arts	Served on staff for eighteen years		Served on staff for eighteen years
Morrow	Electives	Strong advocate for all electives		Coaches volleyball so will not attend fall after-school meetings
Halliday	Special Ed	Knows instruction, willing to advocate for all teachers and students		Not well known across campus
Yoshiaki	Counseling	Knows SEL learning		In second year of counseling
Team Review Questions				
Do the selected team members provide balance in the following areas?	**Grade Levels or Departments** (Yes) or No	**Points of View** (Yes) or No		**Experience Levels** (Yes) or No
Are the members . . .	**Leaders?** (Yes) or No	**Credible?** (Yes) or No	**Willing to Disagree Professionally?** (Yes) or No	**Able to Articulate Ideas Effectively?** (Yes) or No
Where might roadblocks to progress lie?	Mathematics and counseling departments may want staff with more experience. Getting Sorrento to understand this is not going to be like a traditional department chair position could be an issue.			

Figure 2.1: Example form for building the leadership team.

simply to become better at collaborating with one another. This initiative would tell staff they would not be allowed to opt out of collaborating.

To make this key selection, the team needs to honestly assess the district or school and identify what outcome they most want to achieve. Then, they would list factors within their control that are preventing them from accomplishing that outcome. For example, if the district is seeking to create more effective site leaders, the guiding coalition might identify roadblocks such as a lack of a districtwide leadership preparation program, the lack of understanding by principals of how to lead effective PLCs, and a general misunderstanding of the role of the principal in leading the learning on a campus. The district can mitigate all of these factors with meaningful planning. Developing a program to identify potential future administrators and a mentoring program is a first step. The district could construct a program for new principals to complete that includes not only the nuts and bolts of how to build a PLC and lead the learning on a campus, but also visits to sites outside the district that are doing this work well.

At the school level, a guiding coalition may select improving learning for all students through meaningful staff collaboration as its overarching focus. Factors that are currently keeping the school from achieving this may be lack of understanding of the work of the team, lack of common formative assessments, or an inability to react to the data students are producing. The team should not include factors that the school has no control over, such as poverty and lack of parent involvement. Once the team has identified the challenging factors, the members would commence solving those problems. Teaching staff to develop reliable common formative assessments and react to student data will often take more than one year to accomplish, so this focus needs to be sustained over time.

With a focus selected, the guiding coalition of the district or school can set about designing the professional growth plan or selecting strong instructional practices to emphasize for the school year. The leadership team often does not need to look beyond its district or campus borders to find instructional practices that all students would benefit from. One example of this is in Huntsville, Texas, where Gibbs Pre-Kindergarten Center assembled a strong group of administrators, teachers, and academic coaches and then began to consider what knowledge and skills are most essential for every four-year-old exiting their school (J. Anderson, personal communication, November 15, 2019). These conversations took time. After the team explored current research and the professional practices that the hardworking staff at Gibbs were already employing every day, the leadership team selected student notebooks as their emphasis for the year. The schoolwide process was based on a system that one of their teachers was already employing, in isolation, in her classroom. The notebooks would include all the essential learning that students would need to have in place to be successful in kindergarten. Leadership team members led the training of staff and served as key guides on collaborative teams when questions arose. Once the notebooks were implemented in classrooms, students took charge of coloring in their skills as they acquired them. The notebooks became a great source of pride for the students, their parents, and teachers.

This is a great example of a leadership team working collaboratively with their colleagues to build an initiative from the ground up. If the principal had showed up at a staff meeting and announced that Gibbs would be implementing new student learning notebooks, the rollout of the notebooks might have gone faster, but the initiative probably would have faded quickly as the administration forced another idea on the teachers. Time and collaboration for research, building on internal expertise, training, and support ensured success. In this case, Gibbs moved more slowly in order to create lasting, meaningful change.

As the guiding coalition develops the professional growth plan, it can expect several potential issues to come up that, if left unaddressed, will keep the district or school at PLC lite. These potential issues may include, among others, teachers who rarely bring data to their collaborative team meetings, teams that use the time set aside for collaboration to discuss parents or field trips, or staff simply waiting until the meeting is over. The possible issues that might cause a site to fall short of its goals are too numerous to list here. It is important that the guiding coalition do a meaningful, honest audit of why they are not achieving their goal. Jim Collins (2001) would call this "confronting the brutal facts" (p. 70). In order for this to take place, it is important that the guiding coalition meetings be a safe place where everyone feels free to share without fear of repercussions. If the guiding coalition is not coming up with any factors, it may be that the environment is not a place where everyone feels free to collaborate.

An essential aspect of leading as a team is to demonstrate to the rest of the staff that leadership is shared. Jeanne Spiller and Karen Power (2019) state in their book *Leading With Intention*, "Shared leadership is a critical component of school leadership teams" (p. 64). One excellent way to do this is to have members of the guiding coalition lead the professional learning that will be presented throughout the year. Key staff members leading these sessions shows shared leadership because staff provide best practices to their peers. An added benefit to this strategy is that it offers a powerful message to reluctant staff members who take a *wait-and-see* approach when new initiatives or priorities arise. Although they show very little outward resistance to adhering to the principles of PLC and its practices, late-adopting staff members will only buy into the process once it is clear that this is not a passing fad, but real change in how the district or school operates.

The shared-leadership model can be implemented at the site level and district level. However, it takes a leader who is willing to create a collaborative leadership team that has permission to find best practices, explore these practices, and then provide support to the rest of the staff. While this is happening, the leader must be patient and willing to allow members of his or her leadership team to guide their colleagues through the hard work without rushing the collaborative process or abandoning the work altogether.

Anthony Muhammad and Luis Cruz (2019) remind us in the book *Time for Change* that leadership teams should engage in the following activities:

1. To guide and support staff members not on the team so they work together to continuously focus on increasing student learning.

2. To learn, and then share with staff, research-based best practice that aligns with increasing student learning.

3. To actively listen to and provide a source of support for staff members grappling with challenging yet necessary change initiatives. (p. 118)

The kind of peer leadership that Muhammad and Cruz (2019) describe can only come from an empowered, trusted team. A collaborative leader who builds such a team will create a healthier organization with a high rank-and-file morale.

Summary

In this chapter, we've discussed the importance of collaborative leadership in an accountable PLC. While PLC lite might emphasize teachers meeting regularly, true PLCs operate collectively at every level, including within district and school leadership. The best leaders understand they cannot do everything so they work in teams for better results and to set an example for the rest of the organization. The guiding coalition or leadership team must consist of credible leaders who serve as effective messengers of the mission and vision and the PLC process as a whole. Once formed, the guiding coalition takes the lead in maintaining the focus on the collective commitments and developing and executing professional growth plans. The next chapter will take a closer look at staying focused on the mission and vision with a manageable set of collective commitments.

Chapter 2 Discussion Questions

1. Share a time as a leader when you wanted to move forward with an initiative that did not have the support of the rank and file of the district, school, department, or grade level. What were the results? How did you rebuild the trust of the organization's team members?

2. Of the research shared in this chapter, which quote resonates with you the most? Why?

3. What action will you take as a result of that quote to move the organization further down the road toward being an accountable professional learning community?

4. Before you use the reproducible "Building an Effective, Balanced Leadership Team" (page 42), brainstorm some members of the organization that would make good guiding coalition team members. Why did you select these members?

5. After using the reproducible "Building an Effective, Balanced Leadership Team" (page 42), how many of your team members from the list you brainstormed remain good candidates for the guiding coalition?

Chapter 2 Reflection Worksheet

Learning Target

My job after reading this chapter is to collaborate with teacher colleagues to build an effective, focused guiding coalition.

Success Criteria

▸ *I know I have done my job when I can explain some of the key research behind building a guiding coalition.*

▸ *I know I have done my job when I can explain to the guiding coalition why focusing on a few key initiatives is important and how it can affect the entire district or school.*

▸ *I know I have done my job when I can recognize key staff members who will lead others to commit to the PLC process.*

I would restate the learning target for this chapter in this way:

If I had to pick one idea or concept from this chapter that really stands out, it would be:

The concept or idea that sparks my imagination is:

Those imaginative ideas are:

The success criterion that gives me the biggest challenge is:

Steps I can take to help overcome that challenge are:

Building an Effective, Balanced Leadership Team

Possible Team Members	Subject or Grade Level	Assets	Liabilities

Team Review Questions			
Do the selected team members provide balance in the following areas?	**Grade Levels or Departments** Yes or No	**Points of View** Yes or No	**Experience Levels** Yes or No

Are the members . . .	**Leaders?** Yes or No	**Credible?** Yes or No	**Willing to Disagree Professionally?** Yes or No	**Able to Articulate Ideas Effectively?** Yes or No
Where might roadblocks to progress lie?				

"We're Supposed to Focus on a Few Things, but How Do We Decide What They Are?"

It is vital that you become a "meaningful specific" rather than a "wandering generality."

—Zig Ziglar

When districts and schools begin to look at what it takes to move from PLC lite to an accountable PLC, they are confronted with creating clear, meaningful mission and vision statements, helping teams collaborate, building in time for interventions and extensions, creating common formative assessments, and analyzing the data those assessments produce as well as the practices that led to the data. This can be overwhelming, to say the least. Teachers are often left asking, "I know we are supposed to focus on a few things, but how do we decide what they are?"

Sustained focus on a manageable number of initiatives is how an accountable PLC helps students across the board. In short, all staff must commit to becoming great at a few things instead of being mediocre at a lot of things. To accomplish this, a district's or school's collective commitments come into play. Collective commitments define *how*

Learning Target

My job after reading this chapter is to lead staff in the creation of our collective commitments.

Success Criteria

▸ I know I have done my job when I can cite some of the key research behind creating collective commitments.

▸ I know I have done my job when I can explain to a colleague how to lead my staff to develop collective commitments.

▸ I know I have done my job when I can easily recognize the collective commitments in the everyday work of staff members.

the school or district will support and accomplish its mission and vision (DuFour et al., 2016). Collective commitments are a manageable set of adult actions and student skills that every staff member commits to accomplishing or building. When staff commit to regularly communicating with parents or ensuring every lesson begins and ends with a stated learning target, for example, they acknowledge that these best practices belong in every classroom. It is a clear movement to the *we* culture of a PLC. This chapter will explore the importance of fostering commitment to the mission and vision and present guidelines for selecting collective commitments to guide your work.

Committing to the Mission and Vision

Collective commitments work. According to business and finance writer Neil Kokemuller (n.d.) in his article "The Effects of Team Commitment," articulating collective commitments builds shared responsibility among the staff, increases retention of top staff, and improves bottom line results. Kokemuller (n.d.) goes on to say, "Committed employees make decisions that benefit their colleagues, team and organization. Collaboration on projects and work usually leads to better ideas and more effective performance." This is just as true in educational organizations as it is in business.

Collins (2001) goes even further, stating the "notion of preserving your core ideology is a central feature of great companies" (p. 195). Collective commitments clearly lay out the core ideology of an organization. The leader can then support the commitments by holding everyone in the organization accountable to ensuring they honor the commitments. Because the staff came up with the commitments themselves, teachers are more likely to fully invest in working collaboratively to solve issues. Charlene Li (2019) notes this kind of control is vital because a team of people who believe they can control the outcome of their work will fully commit to the work.

 TEACHER PERSPECTIVE

Rachel Lind, who has taught fifth grade and remedial reading, said that prior to establishing a mission and vision, her school said they were a professional learning community, but the teachers did very little together. However, following mission and vision work and the establishment of collective commitments, Mrs. Lind said for the first time the school became a team. Her fifth-grade team committed to writing common lesson plans and assessments, analyzing data together, and sharing the load of extending and intervening collaboratively and this, according to her estimates, allowed her to complete this work 20 percent faster than she would have working alone (R. Lind, personal communication, June 29, 2019).

The leader needs to work with his or her staff to clearly define how they will make their mission and vision statements come to fruition. Before beginning to select those collective commitments, a process we will discuss later in this chapter (page 48), the leader must clearly communicate the importance of commitments to the staff so they understand they will be held accountable for implementing these commitments to the best of their ability.

Selecting a Focused Set of Commitments

Once a district or school has established a clear purpose that will drive their work and what they need to do to make the *why* come true, they must now agree as to how they are going to accomplish their mission and vision. The *how* is an organization's set of collective commitments—student learning outcomes and behaviors that every adult on campus will engage in to ensure all students learn. These commitments will become non-negotiable expectations that will drive the organization forward.

Qualities of Effective Commitments

When drafting or selecting collective commitments, there are several factors that contribute to the quality of the commitments and thus to the likelihood of success. The factors we will discuss are number of commitments, measurability, controllability, and leader enthusiasm.

One key to effective collective commitments is to have a manageable number. If there are too many, the staff will lose track of them and the organization's effort will be diluted. Remember, the goal is to do a few things well rather than many things poorly. When selecting essential standards for an academic course, teams are encouraged to select a few standards that, when mastered, support students' learning moving forward across a broad scope of standards. One should think of collective commitments in the same manner. A few skills, learnings, and behaviors to which everyone can commit will support work in every classroom across the district or school.

According to cognitive science researchers Graeme S. Halford, Rosemary Baker, Julie E. McCredden, and John D. Bain (2005), the number of pieces of information humans can mentally handle while trying to solve a problem is relatively small: four variables are difficult; five are nearly impossible. When there is a larger set of information, people break down large, complex systems into small, manageable chunks. Based on this research, an organization should pay attention not just to limiting the number of commitments, but also how the commitments can be mentally chunked for easy recall. For example, if a school declared six collective commitments, a staff member might consciously or unconsciously group the commitments into two sets of three. One group might consist of classroom behaviors like every lesson beginning and ending with a clear learning target, students talking 50 percent of the time during classroom discussions, and students needing to provide evidence to support any statement. The other group might include three commitments that occur outside of instructional time, such as making contact with parents at least once a week, entering two data points into the grade book every week, and greeting students at the door as they enter. This makes the commitments easier to remember than if he or she needed to remember all six without chunking. Halford and his colleagues' (2005) research shows that if a site comes up with more than four collective commitments that cannot be chunked, it will be difficult for staff to remember the commitments. If no one can remember the commitments, there is almost no chance they will become ingrained in the culture of the school and provide a basis for school improvement.

The commitments need to be measurable to ensure clarity and leaders' ability to assess that they are helping the organization accomplish its stated mission and vision. If a district or school selects commitments that are not easily measurable, it is difficult to draw a direct line between the commitments and improved student success. A staff that commits to collective teacher efficacy is on the right track, but collective efficacy is hard to measure. Ensuring that classroom discussions contain a minimum of 50 percent student talk, on the other hand, is measurable. For example, if the organization reviews their collective commitments and finds that although they are hitting the mark of 50 percent student talk during classroom discussions, student learning is not accelerating, the staff can decide to adjust the commitment—perhaps raising it to 60 percent student talk.

Controllability is another factor to consider in your collective commitments. When selecting commitments, organizations need to focus on things they can control—things that happen inside the classroom and school. While teachers often hope to increase homework completion rates, for example, homework occurs outside the school and is, therefore, outside educators' control. Focusing on skills and behaviors that teachers have little or no influence over will lead to frustration. However, committing to a few student skills or staff behaviors that happen during the school day and that staff can directly influence allows districts or schools to easily measure the adherence to and effects of those commitments.

When it comes to the collective commitments, principals and district administrators need to lead by example and demonstrate their enthusiasm for the commitments. Leaders should reference the commitments in feedback to staff; for example a principal might say, "I really like the way you began and ended your lesson with the learning target. I appreciate your sticking with our collective commitments." Leaders can also demonstrate enthusiasm for the commitments through data. If students are more successful in defining the main idea of a text, the leader can ask the team if this is related to the increased emphasis on students citing text-based evidence. During a staff meeting, the leader can tell the staff about the six phone calls from parents who expressed how much they appreciated the regular communication from the classroom teacher. Robert Iger (2019), former CEO of the Walt Disney Company, reminds leaders "you have to convey your priorities clearly and repeatedly" (p. 229).

Pushing the staff to focus on ensuring all students gain knowledge and skills that will make them successful down the road will require a certain amount of pressure from the learning leader. However, a leader should heed the advice of Janel Keating, White River School District superintendent, that pressure needs to be applied gracefully (J. Keating, personal communication, November 3, 2017). Gordon and Smith (2015) agree with Keating, saying, "as a leader you want to apply pressure, not stress" (p. 145).

To follow this advice, a leader needs to be open to what the staff are saying and feeling. For example, as a principal I scheduled peer observations at the end of January each year. On these days, I hired a band of roving substitute teachers, which allowed all teachers to spend half a day visiting one another's classrooms and giving feedback to their peers. It was a great exercise to share best practices across campus and initiate discussions across grade levels and subject areas. However, these days were not without teacher stress in the forms of creating plans for the substitutes, leaving one's classroom for half a day, and being observed by colleagues.

Most years the benefits outweighed the stress. One year, however, winter arrived early. Our first snow day was before Thanksgiving. During a typical year, we would close school due to winter conditions two or three times. By Christmas break we had missed six days of school. The winter did not let up, and we had three more snow days in early January. As the peer observations approached, the guiding coalition asked me if the peer observations could be postponed. They said they found value in the days, but the teachers were all behind schedule in teaching their standards and were not up to another layer of stress. If I was not being collaborative or wanted to apply pressure ungracefully, I would have said that the observations were planned and the day would continue as scheduled. Instead, we postponed the days for several weeks until teachers felt more comfortable with where their students were in relation to the essential standards they needed to learn. Gracefully applying pressure means making sure that the school adheres to its collective commitments and student learning stays at the center of the *we* culture, but without forgetting that classroom teachers are working hard and doing their best every day.

A Process for Selecting Commitments

As with drafting the mission and vision, selecting the collective commitments should be a collaborative process. The following eight steps provide guidance for building consensus around specific commitments. A more detailed version of this process appears as a reproducible at the end of this chapter (page 56).

1. Review the mission and vision as a team.

2. Remind the staff that the collective commitments define how they will accomplish the mission and vision.

3. Organize the staff into vertical or cross-curricular teams to ensure each group represents various perspectives on the importance of different skills. Form groups of no more than eight people so all members will have the opportunity to contribute. Task each team with identifying no more than three key skills or learning targets students need to achieve by the time they leave the school.

4. Have teams write each skill or learning target on notecards and post the cards on a wall or whiteboard.

5. Combine similar cards. For example, *fundamental math facts* could combine with *basic math.*

6. Use a consensus protocol such as value voting (see page 26) or standing near your top choice to begin identifying the skills or learning that the staff can most get behind. Eliminate the cards that receive the fewest votes. Allow teams to present brief arguments for the remaining options and then hold a revote. Repeat this process until the staff narrow down the skills and learning targets to a maximum of four (to promote easy recollection, as explained on page 45) that all staff can live with.

7. Repeat this exercise for adult behaviors, such as communicating regularly with parents or beginning and ending every lesson with a student-friendly learning target, that the staff will engage in to ensure all students master the agreed-on skills or learning targets.

8. When both exercises reach their conclusion, share what the staff have come to agreement on. Ask the staff one last time to confirm that they all commit to this set of student skills and adult behaviors that they have selected.

Using a collaborative process such as the one outlined in these steps will ensure that the staff understand and support the collective commitments.

Once the organization has established its collective commitments, it should make those commitments public. Sharing the commitments with the public helps stakeholders clearly understand what the district or school stands for. Further, the collective commitments serve as a strong marketing statement for the organization, which is especially applicable in regions where parents have choices in which school they send their children to. A leader could post them on the school's website or print them out poster size, have all adults on campus sign the poster, and hang it in the hallway across from the office.

Finally, the leader should review the collective commitments annually with the staff, perhaps at the end of the school year or just before school resumes in the fall. Teachers should discuss whether the teacher practices and student skills the school or district has chosen to focus on will provide the most help to all students. If yes, then the staff can roll them forward. If not, the leader needs to guide the conversation about adding, replacing, or deleting specific commitments. At the end of the discussion, a simple poll (such as a thumbs-up or a fist-to-five protocol; DuFour et al., 2016) will reveal whether most staff agree or disagree with the proposed change.

Sample Commitments

To help you visualize the results of the process described in the previous section, consider the following examples of collective commitments and how they affect the daily operations of a school.

Desert View Elementary selected the following three student skills as part of their collective commitments.

TEACHER PERSPECTIVE

Teacher Ashley Nicodemus noted that creating collective commitments was extremely important to both her individual practice and the growth of the school as a professional learning community. The commitments helped her team focus their instruction on skills that they knew their students needed to use throughout their academic career. This was especially important since she was part of the kindergarten team. Discussing the commitments—for example, ensuring all students are proficient in taking Cornell-style notes by the end of fifth grade—with vertical teams allowed her to think of the multi-year learning progressions that would need to take place to make each commitment happen. Her team then owned the beginning of the progression—in this case, introducing students to the format of the note-taking system as they were learning the skills to help them read. Mrs. Nicodemus noted the schoolwide work truly built a *we* culture (A. Nicodemus, personal communication, April 28, 2019).

1. Students will become proficient in finding text-based evidence in any subject.

2. Students will master mathematics facts to automaticity in the four basic functions (addition, subtraction, multiplication, and division) from 0 through 12.

3. Students will learn to take notes in Cornell Notes form and will regularly use their notes to review their learning.

When first developing their collective commitments, the staff also selected two adult teaching commitments.

1. Every lesson will have a clear learning target that students have access to throughout the lesson.

2. We will communicate with parents frequently.

The collective commitment that stipulates that every lesson will have an accessible learning target generates a good example of how collective commitments can come to life in a professional learning community. Once DVES selected this commitment, a kindergarten teacher and a first-grade teacher who were working closely together began writing their learning targets with the verbiage *my job is* (instead of with common phrasings like *I can* or *the student will be able to*). They used *my job is* because all their students understood the concept of a job and took that concept very seriously, in the way that only five- and six-year-olds can. This verbiage caught on and soon all the primary teachers began their learning targets with the words *my job is*. They would not have discovered this effective phrasing, which truly embodies their students' perspectives, without the discussions and sharing that stem from collaborative work, even when that work is collaboration that happened outside of one's grade level or subject matter.

Not only did the my-job-is language engage very young students, secondary teachers also implemented it with their students to much success. These high school teachers let students know that "for the next fifty-five minutes your job is to . . ." This sets up a conversation like the following.

Mrs. Rednor: *Nathan, what is your job?*

Nathan (quoting the learning target on the board): *To understand how to graph linear equations.*

Mrs. Rednor: *Okay, please do your job instead of talking about the game tonight. Thank you.*

This example demonstrates the potential of an accountable PLC. Teachers took the commitment seriously, took ownership of it, and improved on it. Note that the principal did not mandate the incorporation of the *my job is* language; it arose organically from the hardworking, caring professionals in the classroom. Leaders need to remember that the *P* in PLC stands for professional: when adults who work in the classroom are treated as such, they come up with solutions better than anything a lone administrator ever could.

During the first annual review of their collective commitments, Desert View staff decided to add a third teacher behavior: "Adults will share the locus of control in their classrooms with the students and the students will consume their own learning data." The ideas for teachers sharing the locus of control and students tracking their own grades both came from staff members sharing their best practices during staff meetings the prior year.

To clarify, *locus of control* is a term originally put forth by Julian Rotter (1954) in the book *Social Learning and Clinical Psychology*. In the context of psychology, internal locus of control means being in control of one's own fate while external locus of control means that fate is beyond one's own control (Rotter, 1954). In the context of the classroom, locus of control refers to who is in control of the classroom. If locus of control in the classroom is shared, the teacher takes on a facilitation role, guiding the students' learning and allowing the students to take control of some simple routines in the classroom.

For example, instead of the classroom teacher sitting at the document camera going over a writing sample he or she created as a model for the class, a student can present his or her own writing as a sample. If the student is a good writer, he or she is a peer model for others. Having a fifteen-year-old explain his or her thinking to peers is a powerful exercise for both the model student and the rest of the class. This form of reciprocal teaching was identified by Hattie (2009) as carrying an effect size of 0.74. Effect size is a measure of how much impact a strategy improves student learning compared to not using it, with 0.74 being a "very high" rating that suggests reciprocal teaching has a significant impact (Hattie, 2009, p. 204). If the model student has not yet reached proficiency, the teacher communicates to the class that everyone can make mistakes and it is okay. In a supportive classroom environment, making the learning

TEACHER PERSPECTIVE

Garth Lind noted that collective commitments helped everything become streamlined. Students were accountable for the school's values and they responded. In short, the students felt like they owned the values that the adults had agreed to (G. Lind, personal communication, June 29, 2019). Rachel Lind also appreciated that everyone on staff committed to the values. She observed that everyone—staff and students alike—was accountable to them (R. Lind, personal communication, June 29, 2019).

process public can be powerful because other students who are not yet proficient will see that they are not alone and that mistakes are part of the learning process. When the teacher cedes the document camera or otherwise shares control with students, it frees the teacher to move through the class, check in with struggling students, and use proximity to manage behavior and time on task. With these benefits, it is easy to see why a school would add shared locus of control to their collective commitments.

Summary

A compelling mission and vision will only go so far. An organization needs to commit to doing the work that will help all students learn as the district or school pushes to becoming an accountable professional learning community. Collective commitments are the day-to-day work that a *we* culture holds everyone accountable to. Collins (2001), Iger (2019), Kokemuller (n.d.), and Li (2019) all note that organizations do better when focused on becoming great at a few things. Working together to ensure all students are learning should be the focal point of every district or school. However, a leader needs to maintain that focus without forgetting the hardworking people trying to implement the work (J. Keating, personal communication, November 3, 2017). Once an organization has selected and implemented its collective commitments, the district or the school will have a clear path to making their mission and vision a reality for all staff and students.

Chapter 3 Discussion Questions

1. What are collective commitments, and how can they support learning for all students?

2. What collective commitments should your district or school have in order to fully support your stated mission and vision?

3. Where might your organization run into resistance when trying to get everyone to commit to a few key student learning and adult behavior initiatives? How can this resistance be handled positively?

4. How will the organization share these collective commitments with all stakeholders?

Chapter 3 Reflection Worksheet

Learning Target

My job after reading this chapter is to lead staff in the creation of our collective commitments.

Success Criteria

▸ *I know I have done my job when I can cite some of the key research behind creating collective commitments.*

▸ *I know I have done my job when I can explain to a colleague how to lead my staff to develop collective commitments.*

▸ *I know I have done my job when I can easily recognize the collective commitments in the everyday work of staff members.*

I would restate the learning target for this chapter in this way:

If I had to pick one idea or concept from this chapter that really stands out, it would be:

The concept or idea that sparks my imagination is:

Those imaginative ideas are:

The success criterion that gives me the biggest challenge is:

Steps I can take to help overcome that challenge are:

Selecting Collective Commitments

The following eight steps serve as a template for a meeting for an organization to create their collective commitments.

1. Review the mission and vision as a team.

2. Remind the staff that the collective commitments define how they will accomplish the mission and vision.

3. Organize the staff into vertical teams. The teams should identify no more than three key skills and learning targets students need to have in place by the time they leave the school. If it is a district leadership team creating collective commitments, they should discuss what the students need to have in place when they leave the district. High school teams should discuss what all students need to have in place when they walk across the stage to receive their diplomas. Middle school and elementary schools should discuss what learning is and what skills all students need to have in place as they matriculate to the next level to ensure success.

   It needs to be made very clear to all those helping to create collective commitments that identified learning and skills will be deemed essential for *all* students. It does not matter if special designations (for example, individual education plan, English learner, 504 plan) are attached to the student's name; all means *all*. If a skill, for example, is vital to success for general education students, then it is equally important that all students acquire this skill as well.

4. Have teams write each skill or learning target on a notecard once the teams come to agreement on the three skills or learning the students will need. No more than one skill or learning per card. Each team then posts the cards on an easily observable flat surface; a white board or wall would do nicely.

5. Combine similar cards. For example, if two groups' notecards say "fundamental math facts" they can easily be combined with another card that says "basic math."

6. Use a consensus protocol such as the value voting protocol from the forty-five-minute mission and vision meeting (see chapter 1, page 26)

page 1 of 2

to identify the skills or learning that the staff can most get behind. If the facilitator wants to use a different protocol, he or she can place the combined cards around the room on a desk or table. Then ask the staff to stand behind the desk or table that represents the skill or learning that the staff member feels provides the most leverage academically for students. Some staff members will point out that if they stand behind a desk or table, they can only vote for one thing. In this case, the facilitator should remind them to use their one vote for something very important.

Regardless of which protocol they use, the will of the group should emerge in a clear, observable manner. If more than three or four skills or learning targets tie, then they should remove cards not involved in the tie. The groups supporting cards still in the running are given two minutes to come up with a thirty-second argument for why everyone should agree with them.

Teams are then allowed to make their arguments and hold a revote. This process can be repeated until the staff narrow down the skills and learning to a maximum of four things the whole staff can live with.

7. Once the collective commitments for student learning are established, repeat the exercise for the adult behaviors that the staff will engage in to ensure all students master the agreed-on guaranteed skills or learning.

8. When both exercises reach their conclusion, share what the staff has come to agreement on. Ask the staff one last time to confirm that they all commit to the set of student skills and adult behaviors they have selected.

"How Do You Find Time to Support Learning When There Are So Many Other Issues to Deal With?"

We follow those who lead not because we have to, but because we want to.

—Simon Sinek

All educators enter the field of childhood education for the same reason: to help children learn. It is that simple. DuFour's (2015) *In Praise of American Educators* clearly builds the case that teachers today are doing a better job of helping students learn than ever before, despite the many, many challenges that are presented every day in every class. However, it is very easy for leaders to lose sight of this success, and to be overwhelmed by the managerial part of the job. One simply needs to look at the email inbox of a district leader or principal to see how many issues, big and small, confront them in a day. If a leader is not careful, that fundamental purpose of helping students learn can be pushed way down the list of things to do. Teachers often see this problem in their schools and wonder how their leaders will find time to support learning when there are so many other issues to deal with.

Learning Target

My job after reading this chapter is to construct a plan to be in classrooms where learning takes place and create a system that allows staff to share their best practices.

Success Criteria

▸ I know I have done my job when I take a meaningful look at my calendar and reorganize my time during the school day to be in classrooms more.

▸ I know I have done my job when I create a system to track which staff I have seen and when.

▸ I know I have done my job when I create a plan for utilizing the best practices of the staff to support the learning of all staff members.

The short answer is to be intentional about knowing what is happening at the classroom level and to trust the professionals who work in the building. When a leader does these two things, he or she will have more bandwidth for supporting learning and collaboration. Managing a district or site will always be part of the job, but one must not lose sight of the main focus—the education of the students in the classrooms. Leaders need to counteract distractors by intentionally scheduling time to spend in classrooms and leveraging teachers' professional expertise. This chapter will provide guidance related to protecting time in classrooms, observing efficiently, sharing best practices, and including all adults.

Protecting Time in Classrooms

According to the first two big ideas of a PLC, the fundamental purpose of the school is to ensure all students learn at high levels. We must work collaboratively and take responsibility for the success of each student (DuFour et al., 2016). For a school principal, this responsibility means supporting students and teachers as the community's instructional leader. As the building instructional leader, it is important to know the teachers' strengths and weaknesses, such as the type of students that teachers connect with easily and those that present challenges for them instruction-ally. The only way principals can truly know and understand their teachers is by being in the classrooms regularly and observing and giving feedback to the teachers. Spending time on campuses is just as important for a district leader. Without face-to-face interaction with teachers and students, it is far too easy to see numbers when one looks at sites rather than the people who work and attend school there every day. Business expert Jon Gordon (2017) refers to these valuable interactions between a leader and his or her team as "leadership by walking around" (p. 108). The barriers of *them* begin to break down and a *we* is built. It is important to members of an organization to see the learning leader in classrooms and receive feedback from that leader. Fundamentally, a professional learning community consists of accountable collaborative teams and a collaborative leader.

Being on campuses and in classrooms allows leaders to better support collabo-rative teams. When a leader sees staff in action assessing students and reacting to the data those assessments produce, he or she will be able to guide and support the discussions of collaborative teams. For a site leader, being in classrooms more means teachers get more frequent feedback, and this helps staff members grow their practice quicker. The more feedback the teachers get, the more engaging their prac-tice becomes. Students learn more and the number of minor discipline issues drops considerably. This further frees up the principal to focus on instructional leadership, as he or she will have fewer behavior referrals to address.

To help the leader focus on learning (the first big idea), he or she should collaborate (the second big idea) with the administrative assistant or similar front office staff to protect time in classrooms. Specifically, the principal or district leader can relinquish some control over his or her calendar to a trusted administrative assistant. It is important to remember that the front office job is very difficult. Dealing with requests from staff and parents, managing attendance, and handling any other issue that may present itself while always putting on a pleasant face for anyone who comes through the front door is challenging. Asking the administrative assistant or other staff members to take on one more thing should not be done haphazardly. Additionally, turning over his or her calendar is a big step for the leader. However, this step helps free the leader to focus on instruction and collaboration and is thus a productive practice.

Business writer Issie Lapowsky (2014) notes that it is not just educational leaders who fail to take the step of turning over certain schedule-management duties. In her article titled "The Most Important Person in Your Office Isn't Who You Think," Lapowsky (2014) notes that business leaders often view taking this kind of step as a loss of control, so they are reticent to take it. However, working with an administrative assistant on a calendar is essential to keeping the leader on time and focused. Having the assistant schedule and prioritize times to be spent on campuses or in classrooms in addition to meetings with parents and other administrators takes a load off the district or school leader's shoulders. In addition, the assistant can hold the leader accountable to the schedule—it is always handy to have a person the leader trusts asking, "Shouldn't you be in classes right now?"

When scheduling, or *calendaring*, time for classroom visits, leaders and administrative assistants should set a weekly goal and schedule blocks of time; the blocks of time do not need to be full days. However, the blocks should add up to fulfill the established time-commitment goal. For example, if the goal is for the learning leader to be in classrooms one day a week, those seven hours can be spread out into eight fifty-two-minute blocks. In a school with a staff of forty-five teachers, a schedule of seven hours per week would allow the principal to visit each teacher multiple times per year to support what he or she is working on. Master teachers might receive six to nine visits in a year, and struggling teachers and first-year teachers twelve to eighteen, providing them the support that will help them grow into true professionals.

In the book *Now We're Talking*, Justin Baeder (2018) suggests that 10 percent of an administrator's time should be spent visiting classrooms. This is a robust schedule that would meet the needs of most teachers. Baeder (2018) goes on to suggest that in larger schools with multiple administrators, each administrator should primarily visit classrooms of teachers he or she is evaluating that year. If administrators do follow Baeder's advice and visit classrooms they evaluate, they also need time to meet with other leaders and discuss what they are seeing in each classroom. This will serve to inform all administrators on campus of where the pockets of excellence are and which teachers need more support. Administrative teams using this model should plan to occasionally visit teachers they are not evaluating (perhaps once a quarter) to ensure inter-rater reliability and communicate to the teachers that the entire leadership team cares about their instruction.

Baeder's (2018) 10 percent model should be maintained by district level administrators as well. Being on campuses communicates to teachers that the district administrators care about what is happening at the classroom level. Discussions with teachers and principals can inform district administrators of each site's greatest needs.

It may seem obvious, but it is essential that the administrative assistant actually put the classroom visitation time on the leader's calendar. The physical appearance of this important activity on a calendar forms an important psychological piece for leaders. Ray Dalio (2017), in his book *Principles*, reminds leaders that crossing items off a checklist serves as both a task reminder and confirmation of what has been done. In this case, marking the calendar and recording the classroom visit dates and times serves the same purpose as Dalio's checklist.

Figure 4.1 is a sample of a form that can enable the weekly calendaring of days in the classroom to support learning. A blank reproducible version of this form appears at the end of the chapter (page 76).

TEACHER PERSPECTIVE

Ashley Nicodemus loved the calendaring of time to allow the learning leader to visit her classroom often. The frequent visits and feedback made her very comfortable teaching, like she was "always on the right path." Mrs. Nicodemus related that while teaching at a previous school she received "zero feedback" and because of air-flow issues teachers were required to keep their doors shut. This made her feel very isolated and she never felt sure she was doing what was right for students. However, when she joined a school where she received frequent feedback and multiple visits from her principal, she became a better teacher. The support and feedback let her know that she was teaching well and was part of a community (A. Nicodemus, personal communication, April 28, 2019).

Goal for time in the classroom this week	Seven hours (420 minutes)
Blocks of time to be in classrooms	Three sections (150 minutes each) Monday 8:15–10:45 Wednesday 12:30–3:00 Thursday 10:00–12:30
Teachers and time in need of support	Mrs. Forel (Morning) Mr. Cassel (Morning) Mr. Brandt (Afternoon) Mrs. Quintana (Afternoon) Mr. Franz (All)

Figure 4.1: Worksheet for calendaring time to be in classrooms.

It is also best practice for a learning leader to keep a record of the day and time of each classroom visit. This will help the leader and administrative assistant track progress toward the weekly time-in-classrooms goal, ensure that each teacher receives an appropriate number of visits, and vary the day and time of visits. Figure 4.2 is an excerpt of such a spreadsheet. In this example, Mr. Yoren is a teacher who has struggled with instructional practices in the past and Mrs. Cassel is a new teacher, so the learning leader on campus visits them more frequently and for longer periods of time.

Teacher	Visit 1	Visit 2	Visit 3	Visit 4	Visit 5
Hagar	8/30 Friday 9:30–10:00	9/16 Monday 8:00–8:20	10/17 Thursday 2:00–2:25	11/12 Tuesday 12:30–1:00	12/17 Tuesday 8:45–9:20
Cassel	8/29 Thursday 12:45–1: 20	9/5 Friday 9:00–9:40	9/16 Monday 10:00–10:30	10/2 Wednesday 1:30–2:15	10/17 Thursday 12:30–1:00
Forel	9/5 Friday 8:20–8:50	10/2 Wednesday 2:15–2:50	11/7 Thursday 11:00–11:30	12/9 Monday 9:35–9:55	1/9 Tuesday 1:10–1:35
Luwin	9/5 Friday 8:57–9:30	10/2 Wednesday 1:00–1:22	11/12 Tuesday 1:05–1:37	12/17 Tuesday 9: 25–9:45	1/9 Tuesday 12:40–1:10
Yoren	8/30 Friday 8:40–9:25	9/3 Wednesday 12:40–1:15	9/19 Thursday 9:15–9:50	10/2 Wednesday 12:15–12:55	10/15 Tuesday 2:00–2:40

Figure 4.2: Tracking classroom visits.

Observing Efficiently

When visiting classrooms, the learning leader needs to be focused and efficient. Even with several hours a week devoted to being in classrooms, the leader's time is still at a premium. In this section, we discuss how you can make the best use of classroom-visit time, including what to look for when observing teachers and how to give concise, constructive feedback.

Focused Observation

When we try to see everything, we miss a lot. A lack of focus will contribute to unfocused feedback, and to a struggling or new teacher unfocused feedback is only slightly better than no feedback. Lisa Carter (2007), author of *Total Instructional Alignment*, provides guidance on this topic. She suggests learning leaders only look for four things when observing instruction (Carter, 2007).

1. **Standards- or objective-based instruction:** Does this instruction clearly link to the standards?

   The first question of a PLC is, What is it we want our students to know and be able to do? (DuFour et al., 2016) and collaborative teams should answer that question by determining which standards are essential for all students to master. This work then pairs with the instruction in the classroom. Every subject area, grade level, and course has some set of standards, whether created at the district, state, or national level. If the instruction is not standards based, the observing administrator should be asking why.

2. **Congruency:** Do the activities being done by the students match the stated learning target?

   Clearly stating what the learner is about to learn before any teaching takes place is a powerful tool, and student learning increases if the target is accessible to students throughout the lesson (Hattie, 2019; Stiggins, 2011). When a leader observes a class, he or she should ensure that the learning target is not only present but matches the activity, and vice versa. This ensures the target is being used productively and not just posted for the sake of compliance. I have seen a classroom where the whiteboard displayed "Learning target: Algebra." This was technically correct, as the students were solving linear equations, but it certainly did not further the students' understanding of what they should take away from the lesson. In another case, a teacher had posted a learning target about the causes of the American Revolution, but the lesson concerned the Civil War. These are extreme examples; more often the teacher begins the lesson focused on the learning target but unintentionally drifts away from it. Feedback from an observation can help rectify this honest mistake.

3. **Diagnostic or prescriptive approach:** Is the instruction diagnosing what the students know or do not know? Is it filling in knowledge the students have demonstrated they are lacking? Is the instruction extending the knowledge the students already possess?

   A lesson might be designed to inform the teacher more about what students know and do not know, or a lesson might be intended to remediate or extend students' knowledge. Either purpose is a valuable use of classroom time and can be vital in supporting students in gaining essential skills or knowledge that are relevant, have endurance, will be assessed, and have the leverage to help student learning down the road (Ainsworth, 2013).

4. **Frequent monitoring:** Is the teacher finding out in real time how students are being successful and how they are struggling as the lesson rolls out?

   How a teacher investigates student needs and responds to those needs on the fly reveals a lot about that person as an instructor. When administrators observe classrooms, they should be on the lookout for these authentic assessments that expert teachers are continually engaging in because they are vital to student success. This can be through large-group or small-group questioning, technology, or one-on-one conferences. In other words, the teacher assesses if the students are meeting the stated learning target, then supports the students' next steps in their learning progression. Informal, ongoing assessment is a very valuable use of class time. If these assessments are missing, the administrator should have a conversation with the teacher at the earliest possible opportunity.

Effective Feedback

After conducting a classroom visit or observation, the leader should give feedback to the teacher based on what he or she observed. This type of feedback should be neutral, not good or bad—just a conversation starter. However, some staff, depending on past experiences, will assume neutral feedback is negative feedback and may react as though they are being criticized. On occasion, there is nothing an administrator can do to prevent this from happening. How a person receives feedback is colored by how he or she views the person giving the feedback. In fact, in the book *Thanks for the Feedback*, authors Doug Stone and Sheila Heen (2014) maintain it is impossible to divorce feedback from the relationship between the feedback giver and receiver. If a leader gives neutral feedback to a staff member that he or she does not have a good relationship with, the teacher is likely to assume the feedback is negative.

Noticing and wondering is a great approach to delivering neutral feedback that prompts teachers to reflect on their practices. This method allows the leader to call attention to (notice) an aspect of a teacher's practice and gently ask (wonder) how the teacher might improve that area, ask for more detail, or prompt a reflective conversation. To offset any potential defensiveness, a leader can begin the feedback with what he or she saw that was a good example of teaching or relationship building. It is beneficial to start the noticing and wondering conversation with an *I like*. Beginning with a statement about what you like in the teacher's practice becomes a small celebration of what is going right in a classroom. Then the leader can mention one thing he or she noticed and one related wondering. For example, when visiting a ninth-grade life sciences classroom, the administrator observes a robust student discussion that features making predictions about how a plant cell may differ from an animal cell, but the lesson lacks a stated learning target that students have access to. After class, the administrator gives the following feedback.

> **Administrator:** *Great class! I liked the classroom discussion, especially how you pushed the students to a high DoK level and gave them room to talk. I noticed there was no learning target that I could see and I wonder if the learning target was available to the students throughout the lesson.*

The administrator then gives the teacher a chance to respond, perhaps as follows.

> **Teacher:** *Thanks for the feedback. The students had a handout on their desks that had the learning target on the front. When you stopped by, they had flipped to the back of the handout. That's why you did not see it, but it was there.*

> **Administrator:** *Great! I figured it was there somewhere. How did you prep the students for that conversation?*

Alternatively, the conversation might proceed this way.

> **Teacher:** *Thanks for the feedback. I'm glad you liked the discussion. But you are right, I forgot to post the learning target. I stated it at the beginning of class, but did not post it.*

> **Administrator:** *Okay. I am glad you stated it, but remember we committed to having the target posted and available throughout every lesson for the*

students to refer to. So, I need you to make sure that happens. How did you prep the students for that conversation?

The *I like, I noticed, I wonder* format allows the leader to celebrate the best practices going on in classrooms and still push forward the teacher's practice through self-reflection. Learning leaders who have used this method are often surprised by how much more willing staff members are to look at their own practices when feedback starts with an *I like* celebration.

This feedback can occur in person, but the leader might also choose to record the feedback on a walkthrough form and email it to the teacher. There are many walk-through forms available, but the leader needs to be sure the form does not become a checklist, which shifts the focus of the visit to a narrow set of behaviors instead of keeping the focus on the actual teaching. In lieu of a checklist, a leader should use an open response feedback form—it might even follow the same *I like, I noticed, I wonder* format. Figure 4.3 shows a sample feedback form; a blank reproducible version appears at the end of this chapter (page 77).

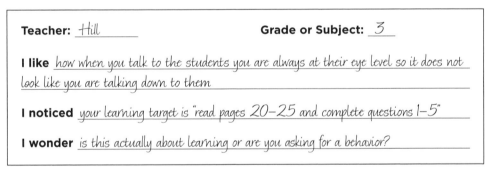

Teacher: Hill   **Grade or Subject:** 3

I like how when you talk to the students you are always at their eye level so it does not look like you are talking down to them

I noticed your learning target is "read pages 20–25 and complete questions 1–5"

I wonder is this actually about learning or are you asking for a behavior?

Figure 4.3: Classroom observation feedback form.

Sharing Best Practices

Helping staff learn and employ educational best practices is a key facet of supporting learning. DuFour and colleagues (2016) assert that "PLCs operate under the assumption that the key to improved learning for students is continuous job-embedded learning for educators" (p. 10). One of the most overlooked resources to support the learning of staff members is the staff itself. Going back to the SUCCESs framework, one of the key components to making an idea or a cultural shift stick is credibility (Heath & Heath, 2008); using staff to share best practices carries a high level of credibility. One place it is relatively easy to share best practices and staff-led professional development is in traditional weekly or biweekly staff meetings.

The regular staff meeting needs to be a vehicle for improving practice instead of a time when the principal doles out information that he or she could easily email. This is not a new idea; Richard DuFour and Robert J. Marzano (2011) strongly suggest using meeting time for staff development in their book *Leaders of Learning*. However, staff development time needs to focus on the collective commitments, not random professional development topics. Staff development meetings should be led by staff members. By being in classrooms regularly, the learning leader can identify staff members who are proficient or expert in transferring the key skills to the students. These staff members would then share their best practices at the regularly scheduled meetings. These professional development meetings carry a lot of weight with staff. Not only do staff tend to be more engaged when a colleague is sharing, they generally do not hesitate with follow-up questions even after the meeting's conclusion.

Another way to share best practices and acknowledge expertise is through peer observations, in which a small group of staff observes the classroom of an expert teacher (see page 78 for a worksheet to guide this process). Susan Fowler (2017), in her book *Why Motivating People Doesn't Work . . . and What Does*, reminds readers that everyone needs to have a sense of competence at work. There is no greater way for a leader to show a teacher that he or she has a high level of competence than to ask him or her to model instructional practices for other staff. Sharing best practices through meetings and peer observations is also itself a form of staff development. By going outside of the guiding coalition to highlight the good work being done across campus, the leader is fostering a new generation of teacher leaders.

TEACHER PERSPECTIVE

First-grade teacher Kara Frazier spoke positively about the change from logistical staff meetings to professional development meetings, saying that they went from "all fluff to something I could use the next day in my classroom." Mrs. Frazier especially liked being given time with her collaborative team to really consider how a best practice would look in her specific class and grade level. Mrs. Frazier said there were several trainings that fellow teachers provided years previously that held up over time, from close-reading strategies, to getting students to quickly master their basic mathematics facts, to the process of notebooking—which not only involves students tracking the data that they produce as they progress through the essential standards, but also setting learning goals for themselves and analyzing their own learning needs. Mrs. Frazier went on to say that when her colleagues began sharing best practices, it felt like the weekly staff meetings really meant something, that they required engagement beyond just attendance (K. Frazier, personal communication, April 17, 2019).

Including All Adults

A final important topic related to instructional leadership and supporting learning is the inclusion of all adults. The importance of ensuring inclusivity for all members of the school community is critical. While this inclusivity can be achieved in obvious ways such as by making time for all staff members to speak during meetings, it also requires the daily maintenance that comes from having a mindset that values inclusivity. In the book *Winning the NFL Way*, authors Bob LaMonte and Robert Shook (2004) relate a story about Andy Reid's time as head coach of the Philadelphia Eagles. LaMonte and Shook (2004) describe a big win, after which Reid's assistant, Carol Wilson, congratulated him when he arrived at work on Monday. Reid replied, "Congratulations to you too, Carol."

Reid was known for this kind of out-of-the-box thinking when it came to recognizing people who are not usually considered part of the team. Butch Buchanico, who ran game-day operations, remembers Reid thanking him for the job he did and asking him to pass on the appreciation to the stadium cleaning crew, hot dog vendors, and plumbers. Reid told Buchanico that they were all part of the Eagles and the players and coaches could not succeed without them. Buchanico shared the kudos with his operations team, who were taken aback—they did not receive thanks from the top of the organization . . . ever (LaMonte & Shook, 2004).

Reid's broad vision of his team is an example of the kind of daily attitude of inclusivity that can have a big positive impact on how people feel and behave. Reid considered the team to be more than the fifty-three players, numerous coaches and assistant coaches, trainers, and scouts that most people think of as a football team. Reid recognized that everyone from the front office staff to the lemonade and beer vendors had a role to play in taking care of the players and the fans to ensure the game-day experience in Philadelphia was as great as it possibly could be. As a result of their leader's inclusivity and collectivist mindset, all members of the organization felt part of the team and more dedicated to its purpose. And the Eagles saw better results, too, earning a berth in the conference championship game four years in a row from 2001 to 2004 and adding a fifth appearance in 2008. Reid continued this inclusive model when he became head coach of the Kansas City Chiefs, and led that team to its first Super Bowl victory in fifty years in 2020.

School leaders need to think more like Reid when considering their staff. School leaders often limit their vision of the school team to teachers and maybe front office staff. Other learning leaders may include paraprofessionals and other aides. Everyone in the school community needs to be part of the professional learning community. But what can be done to make sure all adults on campus are included in the movement?

By shifting one's thinking to include all, a leader can draw support from each corner of the campus. According to Hattie's (2009) research, collective teacher efficacy has a larger effect on student learning (an effect size of 1.57, nearly four times the average impact of all the strategies Hattie studied) than any other variable he studied. *Collective teacher efficacy* is "when teachers believe that the staff is capable of helping students master complex content, fostering students' creativity, and getting students to believe they can do well in school" (Donohoo, 2017, p. 3). Note that this definition does not say "*teachers* are capable," it says, "the *staff* is capable." This is a key distinction. Staff includes teachers, but also paraprofessionals, counselors, front office staff, cafeteria personnel, and custodial employees. In short, collective efficacy includes every adult on campus; every adult a student comes in contact with during the day must believe that the student can learn and become successful in school.

Once this shift in thinking takes place, the leadership team needs to provide effective training to everyone on the three big ideas and four critical questions of a PLC, so staff members can support the work. Forward-thinking leaders should consider how to more effectively draw these other, noncertificated staff members into the school's mission, vision, and collective commitments (DuFour et al., 2016). Are there funds that can be used to support professional learning for noncertificated staff? Is there time during the week when they are not working directly with students and could receive training instead? For example, on early release days, do noncertificated staff stay in the building but have no duties beyond mundane classroom support?

Professional learning sessions will give noncertificated staff a greater understanding of the expectations of the work the teachers are engaging in. These trainings will also clarify for all staff why all students need to learn at high levels and even draw their voices into collaborative conversations. Often these hardworking adults, like the Eagles vendors and plumbers, see themselves as people who work on site but are not really part of the team. When they are included in the vision of the campus, they get excited. Intentionally training and letting nonteachers on staff know they are appreciated builds community, which is of course important to becoming a professional learning community.

It may take some imagination on the leader's part to train these staff members. Consider, for instance, whether time before school is available for fundamental PLC training instead of using it to put up bulletin boards or make copies. When there is a meeting, instead of going over the details of lunch duty schedules or special education support rotations, it would be a better use of time to introduce nonteaching staff to the three big ideas or collective commitments. The leader should put as much thought into training new paraprofessionals, administrative assistants, and so on as he or she does in training new teachers. This effort will be paid back in the work the leader will get from nonteachers on staff who feel trusted and valued as professionals.

To provide meaningful, productive training to noncertificated staff members, leaders should give an overview of what a professional learning community is, explain how it operates, and ask personnel to apply that information to their own jobs. For example, the front office staff should discuss how their duties support the district's or school's focus on student learning. The custodial staff should look at their practices and discuss how high levels of collaboration among themselves and with the teachers and administration will make their jobs run more smoothly. Security staff can track data on negative student behaviors. As a whole, nonteaching staff can discuss questions like, What needs to change in all positions to make the mission and vision of the school happen? How are noncertificated staff supporting the collective commitments the staff have made?

In 2018, I was supporting the work of Roberto and Dr. Francisco Jiménez Elementary School in Santa Maria, California, as they were working to move from PLC lite to becoming a true professional learning community. The leaders overseeing the campus found that as the teachers sought to be more collaborative in their work, the office staff were going through a difficult time as they tried to do their jobs in a vacuum. The leaders decided to provide training for the office staff in basic collaboration fundamentals and goal setting. Three months later, the office staff were still excited about what they had learned and the positive changes in their jobs.

TEACHER PERSPECTIVE

When Ashley Nicodemus and her team were assigned two paraprofessionals to help support their work in kindergarten, her team immediately worked to integrate the classified staff members into their collaborative team and their mission of making sure all students were successful with the grade-level content by the end of the year. This required working with the administration to rework the paraprofessionals' schedules so the paras could attend collaborative team meetings. Mrs. Nicodemus commented, "I don't know how to not include them in the collaborative team meeting." She went on to say the paraprofessionals hold down a big part of the work, so they need to give input at the collaborative meetings. Mrs. Nicodemus continued to say that if the team wanted the kindergarten students to learn in the most effective way the team needed to use its resources in the most effective way. Often the teachers would take the students most in need of intervention and extension, while the paraprofessionals supported those students who needed more practice. This kind of flexibility could not be effective without making the paraprofessionals partners in the collaborative process (A. Nicodemus, personal communication, April 28, 2019).

They were working better as a team and had improved their ability to support one another. Those skills became vital when one office staff member went on maternity leave and another was hospitalized for a few weeks, leaving the front office missing 40 percent of its staff.

The office staff at Jiménez Elementary appreciated the collaboration fundamentals that they had been trained on and wanted to know what more they could do to support the administrators, teachers, students, and one another. They wanted to be valued and involved. They wanted to feel as though they made a difference by supporting the students they saw every day. After receiving two days of training on the research around why PLCs provide the best opportunity for students to be successful in school, the front office staff fundamentally changed how they saw their jobs and their place in the community that supports student learning.

Summary

By applying the ideas of Baeder (2018) and Lapowsky (2014), the learning leader can prioritize spending time in classrooms and giving feedback to staff to support their work with students. That feedback, when given in a simple format that stimulates discussion, supports best practices and teacher development. DuFour and Marzano (2011) and Fowler (2017) strongly recommend that staff train one another on the strategies and techniques that are producing the best results in their classrooms. However, the learning leader should not limit feedback and training to just certificated teachers. As the story of Andy Reid (page 69) shows, including all members of the organization in the team changes the perspective of those who have felt ignored in the past. This can be done in a district or school by providing intentional training on PLC processes, the mission, the vision, and the collective commitments to staff members typically not included in this work, building a larger *we* to support students.

Chapter 4 Discussion Questions

1. What protocols do we need to have in place to schedule and protect time in classrooms?

2. What changes do we need to make to our staff meetings to make them adult learning centered? What best practices need to be shared with all staff?

3. What could peer observations accomplish for our staff? What steps do we need to take to make peer observations happen?

4. How do we involve all adults in ensuring all students learn at high levels? How will we include nonteachers in the collaborative culture of the organization?

Chapter 4 Reflection Worksheet

Learning Target

My job after reading this chapter is to construct a plan to be in classrooms where learning takes place and create a system that allows staff to share best practices.

Success Criteria

▸ *I know I have done my job when I take a meaningful look at my calendar and reorganize my time during the school day to be in classrooms more.*

▸ *I know I have done my job when I create a system to track which staff I have seen and when.*

▸ *I know I have done my job when I create a plan for utilizing the best practices of the staff to support the learning of all staff members.*

I would restate the learning target for this chapter in this way:

If I had to pick one idea or concept from this chapter that really stands out, it would be:

The concept or idea that sparks my imagination is:

Those imaginative ideas are:

The success criterion that gives me the biggest challenge is:

Steps I can take to help overcome that challenge are:

Worksheet for Calendaring Time to Be in Classrooms

Week of _____ (date)

Goal for time spent in the classroom this week: _____ (hours)

Blocks of time allotted

Day	Time

Teachers in need of support

Name	Day and time to observe

I Like, I Noticed, I Wonder
Feedback Form

Teacher:

Grade or Subject:

I like

I noticed

I wonder

Peer Observation Form

Teacher being observed:

Grade or subject:

Teacher observing:

Grade or subject:

Learning target:

Success criteria:

Number of teacher questions asked of whole group:

Number of teacher questions asked of individual students:

Complexity of questions:

What I was surprised by most:

What I want to use in my classroom:

Additional comments:

"Won't We Just Move On to Something Else Next Year?"

What you stay focused on will grow.

—Roy T. Bennet

Every year, teachers return to their schools bracing for the first staff meeting and fearing their principals will utter the words that strike dread into their hearts: "Over the summer I've been to a conference, so this year we will . . ." They fear this message because it communicates to them that their efforts during the previous year no longer matter. The target has just been moved. They must now learn a new system or protocol that will be the school's focus for the next nine months. Then, most likely, this new thing will also be forgotten for the next thing and the target will move again. And so on and so on . . .

Imagine a site that commits to becoming an accountable professional learning community. The staff and administration work very hard to unpack and select essential standards. Teams build common formative and summative assessments and learn to develop plans for students who are not yet

Learning Target

My job after reading this chapter is to create a plan for carrying forward the collective commitments and sustaining the professional learning plan.

Success Criteria

▸ I can identify the danger of cycling through a great new initiative each year.

▸ I can explain to a colleague the key research behind sustaining a few key initiatives over multiple school years.

▸ I can complete an administrative review for the school year and use the information from the review to inform the professional learning plan.

proficient and plans for meaningful extensions for students who have demonstrated proficiency. Then, after all of that learning and work, teachers show up the following August and hear "So, forget everything we worked on last year." At worst there would be a mutiny; at best staff would grumble to themselves and docilely accept the obligatory one-year initiative.

This lack of focus from one year to the next can easily derail an organization's shift to a *we* culture. If members of the organization feel as though this initiative will be abandoned sooner or later, then they are unlikely to change site or classroom practices, because next year the emphasis will be on something else altogether. This is one of the major arguments staff will use for retaining a *me* culture. Only sustained work over multiple years will get them to buy into a *we* culture.

Unfortunately, this scenario is not that far-fetched. For years, districts and schools have been caught in a cycle of Last Year's Great Initiative and This Year's Great Initiative. In this cycle, each new year brings a new program or professional learning focus that purports to cause all students to love school and make all teachers' jobs so easy they discover an abundance of extra time. Alas, in 180 school days this year's great initiative will become last year's great initiative and the organization will move on to the next shiny object.

It is only when a staff commits to a few key initiatives over multiple years that those initiatives can refreeze, as Lewin (1947; Hattangadi, 2016) put it, and become part of the culture of the district or school. To truly reap the benefits that collaboration brings takes years as teams become accountable to one another and proficient at writing assessments and interpreting student data. For this to happen, districts and schools need to fight the cycle of last year's great initiative and this year's great initiative. In this chapter, we will review methods for staying focused and aligning other initiatives with the PLC process.

TEACHER PERSPECTIVE

Ashley Nicodemus said that keeping the same collective commitments over multiple years was very important. She said, "having a focus brought us together on some sort of common ground." She went on to say that teaching can become very "islandy" where each classroom can feel isolated. With no common ground, teachers may not be completely honest with their colleagues about the practices in their classroom or the conditions under which they give assessments. However, when the whole school is working on the same things there is no reason not to be honest and Mrs. Nicodemus emphasized that the biggest roadblock to true collaboration is dishonesty (A. Nicodemus, personal communication, April 28, 2019).

Staying Focused

In August of 2019, White River School District Superintendent Janel Keating was part of a panel discussion at a Solution Tree Professional Learning Community at Work Institute. During the panel, an audience member asked how she keeps her district focused on their collaborative work. She responded by saying she sends out a welcome-back letter to all staff members every year. In that letter she includes a reminder: "If you wonder what we are doing this year, it's the same damn thing" (Keating et al., 2019). A very clear, easy-to-remember statement informs the whole district that staff are committed to becoming great at the PLC process, not the cycle of yearly new initiatives.

Aside from reassuring staff, there are additional benefits to focusing on becoming a professional learning community and limiting other initiatives. By carrying forward the mission and vision and the collective commitments the staff make from one year to the next, the leader increases the staff's ability to focus on these key initiatives. This is very important according to business turnaround expert Gordon Tredgold (2017), who maintains that increased focus helps staff in three ways.

1. **Building momentum:** Increased focus improves efficacy and thus speeds the rate of progress.

2. **Reducing stress:** Focus eliminates the stress of having too many options or too many things to do.

3. **Increasing engagement:** A clear goal with a focused set of initiatives working toward it prevents staff frustration that might cause them to disengage.

Corporate strategist Eric Holtzclaw (2012) agrees with Tredgold (2017). In his article *The Power of Consistency: 5 Rules*, Holtzclaw (2012) maintains that consistency allows for measuring growth and creates accountability within an organization, both of which can support a district or school in building momentum. Holtzclaw goes on to say that consistency builds a reputation and message for an organization. Applied to a school or district, consistency and focus lead to a reputation that student learning comes first—certainly an admirable goal.

When staff return from summer break to hear the leader announce that there are no new initiatives (one does not have to phrase it as colorfully as Keating [2019]), it will help build momentum, reduce teacher stress, and increase engagement in perfecting new skills. Instead of being distracted by shiny objects, the organization will work on improving its implementation of the PLC process so collaborative teams become more interdependent, formative assessments are clearer, and teachers use information produced by the assessments more effectively. When the leader doubles down on the mission, vision, and collective commitments the organization made the previous year, it honors the work staff members put into learning the commitments and encourages them to go deeper on how to make the commitments impact every student. It is in these commitments that a district or school finds what it stands for. Gordon and Smith (2015) support this way of focused thinking when they say, "What you stand for drives everything else" (p. 11). The right collective commitments lead an organization right to the first big idea of a PLC—focus on student learning (DuFour et al., 2016).

Author and leadership strategist Greg McKeown (2014) agrees that focusing on less will create greater results: "It's true doing less can be harder, both in art and in life. Every word, every scene, every activity must count for more" (p. 160). When this is applied to an educational setting, it means there must be a clear understanding from the leader on down that these few collective commitments can make such a difference that they deserve and require extra and continued attention. Similarly, Gary Keller and Jay Papasan (2013) remind us in their book *The ONE Thing*, "extraordinary results happen only when you give the best you have to become the best you can be at your most important work" (p. 188). That most important work needs to be committing to becoming a professional learning community and the collective commitments that that staff make to their students, parents, and each other.

To assure staff their focused work is making a difference, the learning leader can begin each year with a "state of the school" presentation. The presentation should

TEACHER PERSPECTIVE

Melissa Purswell noted collective commitments that sustain over time can be implemented with any curriculum, at any grade level, in any classroom, in any building. She said implementing and improving practices around the collective commitments not only improved teaching of the curriculum but gave focus to their collaborative groups. The fact that the leadership team helped to create or identify the commitments only empowered the teachers more. Ms. Purswell went on to say, "We weren't creating anything new; we were fine-tuning what we did well and committing as a building to the foundation that started in kindergarten and increased in rigor as the students moved up in the grade levels. Without a doubt so much of our success at DVES can be attributed to our dedication to implementing and holding one another accountable to the commitments. I honestly believe that creating non-negotiables is what saves us teachers from burn-out. We aren't spinning our wheels or jumping on the 'what's the latest and greatest' bandwagon" (M. Purswell, personal communication, November 30, 2019).

open with the mission and vision of the school and a quick review of the collective commitments. The leader can include positive student and parent survey results, significant student academic growth, or improvement in student behavior. The leader should also invite staff to share what the shift to a *we* culture has meant to their practice. This can occur either in a whole-staff setting with presentations from each subject or grade collaborative team or in a small-group setting with staff from several collaborative teams.

To add an interactive element, the leader can write the mission, vision, and each collective commitment on poster paper and have staff move from one poster to the next commenting on how each element helped improve their practice, helped more students learn, or made their jobs easier. Once all staff have visited each poster, the leader can call them back together and re-emphasize that the goal this year is getting better at actualizing the mission and vision, carrying the collective commitments forward, and becoming more effective collaborators and more agile in reacting to student data. These activities will re-energize returning staff and begin to familiarize those new to the district or school with the *we* culture of the organization.

Aligning Other Initiatives With the PLC Process

Make no mistake—after a district or school commits to the PLC process, the rest of the educational world will continue to turn. Mandates will come from the state and federal government; new initiatives will be thrown at leaders from those above them. It is up to the leader to act as a buffer for the rest of the organization. Part of being a leader is defining what is important and necessary and what is not. Leaders must deflect unnecessary distractions. If something comes along that it is essential, it should be addressed within the context of the established collective commitments.

For example, when Hermiston School District in Hermiston, Oregon, asked each of its schools to investigate an underperforming subgroup and create a plan to address the need, DVES, as an accountable PLC school, approached this task within their PLC structure and commitments (F. Maiocco, personal communication, June 29, 2014). The school looked at the student data produced over three years and identified that English learners (ELs) were not performing as well as their peers from other subgroups. The school's guiding coalition then reaffirmed the collective commitments—mathematics-fact fluency, clear learning targets, and shared locus of control—and researched how they would help underperforming ELs. The team also located research about how better communication with parents can help these students by supporting higher expectations and aspirations at home (Hattie, 2009) and how to overcome key factors that keep parents of nonnative-speaking students from partnering with the school (Shim, 2013). Those findings were shared with the staff, who were then trained on how the collective commitments could support ELs. The guiding coalition members provided professional development to deepen staff knowledge about the difference between BICS (Basic Interpersonal Communication Skills) and CALP (Cognitive Academic Language Proficiency) language and the three tiers of language (Calderón et al., 2016). The training ended with staff sharing strategies to encourage students to use academic language and words with multiple meanings in peer discussions and when ELs were serving as student exemplars.

TEACHER PERSPECTIVE

Kara Frazier said the ability to disagree professionally must be part of the collaborative process. She recalled that she had once served on a team that was not confident in the collective commitments of the school, but team members did not want to voice any disagreement. This led to unresolved conflict simmering beneath the surface, which resulted in unnecessary drama and kept the team from doing what is best for all students (K. Frazier, personal communication, April 17, 2019). To avoid this, leaders should often attend collaborative meetings—usually when tension is percolating on a team it becomes palpable during the meeting. Leaders should conduct frank individual conversations with team members to reveal issues. The leader can then follow up by talking to the team about the issues to help resolve them and move the important collaborative work forward.

This work was directly related to the site's collective commitments, one of which was sharing the locus of control of the classroom with all students. Thus, it was important that every student could engage in academic discourse. Understanding how ELs process and use language was also important to a second collective commitment that all students support all claims with text-based evidence. By retaining the work staff had already done (building a collaborative culture, establishing professional practices guided by collective commitments and student learning, confronting uncomfortable student data) and aligning new tasks to existing priorities, the school was able to meet the valid request from the district without compromising the staff's collective commitments.

In addition to meeting the reasonable expectations of a supervising entity (the state in the case of a district or the district in the case of a school), the learning leader and guiding coalition need to search for ways to deepen the learning and improve the practices of their staff over time. An end-of-year collaborative review of successes and challenges will bring a balanced discussion of how the year went and what the district or school should do to continue supporting the learning of staff and students alike. When planning for the following year, it is important that the organization continue to think deeper, not wider. Look to improve or deepen existing initiatives rather than adding new ones. Identify the next steps to continue building the *we* culture of your PLC and improve practices that support the collective commitments.

Figure 5.1 (page 86) shows a form for reviewing what has gone well over the last school year and planning how new learning can advance professional practices without blurring the focus of the organization on their collective commitments. A blank reproducible version of this form appears at the end of this chapter (page 92).

Leaders should note in their plan for advancing the collective commitments that merely establishing them is a major accomplishment worthy of celebration. But don't stop there. Learning leaders should use the same SMART-goal format that collaborative teams use for their goals (see chapter 6, page 100). This will serve as a model for the collaborative teams for how to pick one essential standard to focus on during a school year. If the guiding coalition, with input from the whole staff, selects and shares next year's goal and plan at the end of the school year, they illustrate for staff that what they worked so hard on this year will have a clear through-line into next year. Next year's great initiative will be the same as this year's great initiative. Sharing the professional learning plan in advance communicates to staff that they will continue working on getting better at their collective commitments. Their professional growth will not be subject to an administrative whim; instead, it is a well-thought-out piece of a long-term professional growth plan, with student success at its heart.

Tracking Data Over Time

One of the major tenets of becoming a PLC is staff-driven action research to inform the teams' instruction. *Action research* is when a person or organization seeks transformative change by simultaneously doing research and acting on the results produced by the research. Teachers can compile action research as they track their own student data. They then save these data in order to review them over successive years to determine instructional trends. Which learning targets do the teams teach well? Which essential standards and learning targets do students struggle with? This is research at the most actionable level.

In schools, data are everywhere, but this raw information is useless without refinement. The first step in the refinement process is tracking student data over time. Fred Maiocco, former superintendent of Hermiston School District, once told me that one year is not a trend (F. Maiocco, personal communication, June 29, 2014).

Administrator Year in Review

Major accomplishments: *Establishment of collective commitments for student learning and adult behaviors that all staff committed to*

Professional development that led to accomplishments: *Book study on Time for Change by Muhammad and Cruz*

Internal PD led by staff members

Article Study on "If Lasers Were Bigger Cats Would Catch Them"

Plan to celebrate accomplishments: *"We Did It!" certificates presented at year-in-review staff meeting*

Toast at end-of-year family BBQ

SMART goal for next year to extend this year's accomplishments:
By May, 100 percent of students, when prompted, will be able to explain how the focus of the lesson will help them with 95 percent accuracy.

Professional learning needed to improve or extend this year's accomplishments into next year: *Articles on sharing learning targets*

Possible book study on best practices for sharing learning targets with students

Identify staff with best practices for constructing learning targets to share with staff

Reach out to district coaches for staff at other sites who can share with our staff

Dates for professional learning to take place: *August 20 (half day)*

Once a month at Thursday afternoon staff meeting September, October, November, January

Date for sharing out plan: *At Thursday afternoon staff meeting, May 11*

Figure 5.1: Year-in-review reflection and planning form.

He was absolutely correct. However, if teams track and review data over multiple years over multiple cohorts of students, instructional trends can become very clear. In order for that to happen, teams need to keep data from year to year. Often when I work with collaborative teams, I ask them if the current year's data are in line with what they have observed over the past few years. Rarely do I get any response other than a vague feeling from a team member or two. By keeping the data in a repository, which has become much easier with the advent of digital cloud-based storage, teams can easily engage in longitudinal research instead of guessing. This allows the district or site to be agile in responding to needs and reaffirms and protects what the organization is doing well. Thus, the school can stay focused and continue the right work with confidence. Figure 5.2 (page 88) is an example of a form for tracking data over multiple years. A blank reproducible version appears at the end of the chapter (page 94).

Summary

The cycle of this year's great initiative and next year's great initiative needs to be broken—recall McKeown's (2014) and Tredgold's (2017) recommendations for consistency and Keating's (2019) straightforward wisdom. Districts and schools need to become great at a few things that help all students be successful, and doing so takes sustained effort over multiple school years. When an overseeing agency passes down new initiatives, the learning leader needs to find a way to align the new initiatives with the work that is already being done. A formal data-tracking process will support the learning of each student cohort and provide a picture of school and collaborative team successes and challenges over multiple years.

Essential standard in student-friendly language: (RI.7.1) Students will be able to cite several pieces of evidence to support what is stated and what is inferred.

Dates taught year 1: August 29–September 28

Dates taught year 2: September 4–October 2

Dates taught year 3: September 16–October 4

Dates taught year 4: August 27–September 18

	Number of Students Demonstrating Mastery				Number of Students Demonstrating Proficiency				Number of Students Approaching Proficiency				Number of Students Far from Proficient			
Year	1	2	3	4	1	2	3	4	1	2	3	4	1	2	3	4
Learning Target 1	18	12	10	17	27	31	20	9	21	20	30	27	13	11	23	27
Learning Target 2	20	11	10	17	24	34	15	6	21	20	33	26	14	9	25	31
Learning Target 3	6	3	2	11	20	28	13	8	29	22	37	19	24	21	31	42
Learning Target 4	2	2	2	6	25	29	8	10	29	14	39	16	23	29	34	48
Learning Target 5	20	13	9	16	28	32	23	14	20	18	28	32	10	11	22	22

Conclusions Based on the Data

What is working: Students perform better on learning targets 1, 2, and 5.

Students perform better when the unit is at least twenty-one days so the targets can be taught more richly.

Students performed best on learning target 5 (the one with kinesthetic activities) year in and year out.

Where challenges are: Students had challenges on learning targets 3 and 4.

Students did not perform as well when this was the second essential standard taught.

How we will use these data: In our lesson plans for next year, this will be the first essential standard we will teach.

We will plan a minimum of 21 days for the unit.

We will redesign the lessons that go with learning targets 3 and 4 to include more kinesthetic activities and small group work. We will also write another common formative assessment for each target so we can respond to student needs more quickly.

Source for standard: National Governors Association Center for Best Practices [NGA] & Council of Chief State School Officers [CCSSO], 2010.

Figure 5.2: Tracking student learning data over time.

Chapter 5 Discussion Questions

1. As an organization, have we fallen victim to the cycle of last year's great initiative and this year's great initiative? Share a story from your career when you have been surprised by a sudden shift in the priorities of an organization you worked for.

2. What was our great initiative this year? Does it fit with what we have learned? If it does, how do we continue getting better at it? If it does not, what should we focus on to help more students learn?

3. What do we need to do to create a multiyear plan for professional learning that is related to our collective commitments?

4. How will we defend our key collective commitments from outside forces that threaten to divide our focus?

Chapter 5 Reflection Worksheet

Learning Target

My job after reading this chapter is to create a plan for carrying forward the collective commitments and sustaining the professional learning plan.

Success Criteria

▸ *I can identify the danger of cycling through a great new initiative each year.*

▸ *I can explain to a colleague the key research behind sustaining a few key initiatives over multiple school years.*

▸ *I can complete an administrative review for the school year and use the information from the review to inform the professional learning plan.*

I would restate the learning target for this chapter in this way:

If I had to pick one idea or concept from this chapter that really stands out it would be:

The concept or idea that sparks my imagination is:

Those imaginative ideas are:

The success criterion that gives me the biggest challenge is:

Steps I can take to help overcome that challenge are:

Professional Learning Plan Review

Major accomplishments:

Professional development that led to accomplishments:

Plan to celebrate accomplishments:

SMART goal for next year to extend this year's accomplishments:

Professional learning needed to improve or extend this year's accomplishments into next year:

Dates for professional learning to take place:

Date for sharing plan:

Form for Tracking Data Over Time

Essential standard in student-friendly language:

Dates taught year 1:

Dates taught year 2:

Dates taught year 3:

Dates taught year 4:

Year	Number of Students Demonstrating Mastery				Number of Students Demonstrating Proficiency				Number of Students Approaching Proficiency				Number of Students Far From Proficient			
	1	**2**	**3**	**4**	**1**	**2**	**3**	**4**	**1**	**2**	**3**	**4**	**1**	**2**	**3**	**4**
Learning Target 1																
Learning Target 2																
Learning Target 3																
Learning Target 4																
Learning Target 5																

Conclusions Based on the Data

What is working:

Where challenges are:

How we will use these data:

"How Do We Know If We're on the Right Track?"

The more visible the victories are the more they help the change process. What you don't know about is not a win.

—John Kotter and Dan Cohen

How do we know we are on the right track? The answer to this often-asked question may be simpler than most imagine. Look at where you have been and where you are heading as a district or school. By checking markers along the road to becoming an accountable PLC, teams will be able to celebrate their growth and envision future challenges to be bested.

It is important that an organization advances as a team. The definition of a team is "a group of people working together *interdependently* to achieve a *common goal* for which members are *mutually accountable*" (DuFour et al., 2016, p. 42). It is the common goal that provides the vision of what a district or school can become. That is why goal setting is the fourth pillar of an accountable PLC (DuFour et al., 2016). When teams create goals, those goals serve as targets and timelines for their work. When teams reach goals, the organization should celebrate. Big or small, a

Learning Target

My job after reading this chapter is to gain an understanding of the integral parts setting goals and celebrating progress play in making positive changes to an organization.

Success Criteria

▸ I can explain why goal setting as an organization is important to its long-term growth.

▸ I understand the role celebrating small wins can play in improving classroom practices.

▸ I work with the guiding coalition to set goals for the organization and plan celebrations for the staff which will create a greater sense of community.

celebration marks the achievement of a target and reinvigorates people to grind on to the next marker. If a team fails to meet a goal, the team should examine the reasons, reassess the current reality, and keep working.

Setting Goals

As a high school wrestling coach, at the first practice of the season, I would tell the student-athletes that "a dream is just a dream, until you write it down. Then it becomes a goal. Something real, something you can achieve." I then charged each wrestler to write a goal for his or her own success and one for the team to accomplish together. When everyone came back together, we would come to agreement on the team goal and share everyone's individual goals. The goals, both team and individual, were posted for everyone to see. Each team member was responsible for helping his or her teammates reach their personal goals. By working together to accomplish individual goals, they met their team goals.

The analogy of a wrestling team and a staff of educators works very well. Wrestling and teaching can both be lonely, often individual pursuits that will test one's mental strength and often physical endurance. The most successful wrestling teams and educational organizations have found the key to empowering everyone to reach team goals is by striving for individual goals. Like wrestling, getting everyone in the educational organization to change his or her viewpoint from individualism to collectivism requires a fundamental shift in thinking. Creating goals facilitates this change of perspective. The science teacher is more likely to reach an individual goal when working with all of the science teachers. The science teachers will have an easier time getting students to proficiency in science when working in concert with the mathematics teachers, who, in turn, will find higher levels of student achievement when collaborating with the English and physical education departments. Fifth-grade students will be more successful when their teachers are working with the fourth-grade teachers, and so on.

Routine goal setting is important for teams to do together. In Eric Coryell's (2019) book *Revolutionize Teamwork: How to Create and Lead Accountable Teams*, he states that a team's "conviction comes from a clear and meaningful purpose and a shared fate among team members that connects their individual success or failure to those of their teammates and their team" (p. 109). A meaningful, team-created goal will provide this sense of connection and shared purpose. Once a goal is stated, everyone in the organization is responsible for making it come to fruition.

Team goals should align directly with what the larger organization believes students will need to be successful, creating a single unifying idea that will drive an organization's work forward (Collins, 2001). In a district's case, a goal could be created around retaining their best teachers or improving teacher satisfaction. A school could set a goal around improving students' ability to cite text-based evidence, having more students reading at grade level, or ensuring all students understand fraction-decimal equivalencies. A team should set goals around the essential learning or skills each student needs to acquire during a given course or grade to be successful. Consider the following example of aligned goals.

- **District goal:** By 2025, our district will have eliminated all achievement gaps (socioeconomic, race, and gender) in mathematics.

- **Elementary school goal:** By June 2021, all students leaving fifth grade will demonstrate proficiency on the four basic mathematical functions (addition, subtraction, multiplication, and division) through the tens with 100 percent accuracy.

- **First-grade team goal:** By June 2021, all first-grade students will be able to complete addition problems with addends up through ten with 85 percent accuracy.

- **Middle school goal:** By June 2021, all students will be prepared to enroll in and successfully complete basic algebra at the high school level.

- **Seventh-grade team goal:** By June 2021, all students will improve at least one level of proficiency on the team-created rubric or achieve a perfect score on the common summative assessment on fractions.

- **High school goal:** By June 2021, the percentage of students successfully completing basic algebra on the first attempt will increase by 15 percent over 2020.

- **Ninth-grade team goal**: By June 2021, all students will improve a minimum of one level of proficiency on the team-created rubric or achieve a perfect score on the common summative assessment on linear equations.

Once the organization or team picks its goal, members need to have a conversation about what they need to do to ensure they reach the goal. It is also helpful for the organization or team to create a list of what current practices may impede it from reaching this goal. Collins (2001) calls this a *stop doing list*. It is a tool to identify unproductive practices, but of course the organization must then actually stop doing the things on the list. This may seem like redundant common sense, but many organizations and teams create this list yet continue with unproductive practices just because that is the way it was always done. Avoiding the comforting distraction of unproductive practices is the only way to move forward toward the goal.

During a keynote address delivered at a PLC Institute in Anaheim, California, Richard DuFour (2014) said "every team needs a goal." This simple, short statement provides a lot of direction for leaders trying to develop professional learning communities. In business, in sports, or in schools, goals serve as waypoints along the road that an organization will travel. Long-term goals calibrate an organization. A collaborative team's goal might be a five-year goal for a district or a yearlong goal for student learning. Short-term goals serve to ensure the team is progressing toward the established long-term goal. For example, a five-year goal should launch with a thirty-day goal, followed by a sixty-day goal, and then a ninety-day goal. From there an organization can stretch out to a six-month goal to ensure the district or school is progressing towards the long-term goal. Yearlong collaborative team goals should also have shorter-term waypoint goals. Goals set every six to nine weeks allow teams to judge their progress. The following sections provide more detail about yearlong goals; thirty-, sixty-, and ninety-day goals; and the SMART goal format.

Yearlong Goals

When organizations and teams set their yearlong goals, they are declaring their focus for the year. The yearlong goal for a school or district should be focused on one area that will create growth in the adults' practice that will lead directly to student learning. To find this focus, an organization needs to confront its student learning data honestly. Do English learners perform at a consistently lower level than other students? Do male students achieve proficiency at a significantly lower rate than their female peers in ELA? Is there a research-based instructional strategy that few teachers are using? These questions and others like them would lead to meaningful yearlong goals for an organization. Consider the following examples.

- By May of next year, English learners will achieve proficiency on the state assessment at a rate within 5 percent of their native-speaking peers.

- By June of next year, male students will demonstrate proficiency on the English language arts end-of-unit assessments at a rate that is equal to their female classmates.

- By June of next year, 100 percent of teachers will begin and end each lesson with a review of the learning target and students will have access to the target throughout their lesson.

Thirty-, Sixty-, and Ninety-Day Goals

Kramer and Schuhl (2017), in their book *School Improvement for All*, state that "goals help monitor progress along the way" (p. 17). That is the function of the thirty-, sixty-, and ninety-day goals. They are incremental steps to ensure organizations and teams stay focused and make progress on their yearlong goals. Thirty-, sixty-, and ninety-day goals also serve as opportunities for course correction if teams veer away from what needs to happen to ensure the yearlong goal is reached. Consider the following set of short-term goals related to the yearlong goal, "By June of next year, 100 percent of teachers will begin and end each lesson with a review of the learning target and students will have access to the target throughout their lesson."

- **Thirty-day goal:** By September 25, all staff will be trained on the effect clear learning targets have on student learning and how to write and use effective learning targets.

- **Sixty-day goal:** By October 31, all staff will have a clearly written learning target posted where the students have access to the target throughout the lesson 100 percent of the time.

- **Ninety-day goal:** By December 17, all collaborative teams will use common learning targets.

With this incremental process, leaders train the staff on why learning targets are important and then staff begin to work creating the targets. Once staff are more proficient at writing the targets, then they work on bringing the targets to the front of the students' minds. For the last part of the first semester, staff will work collaboratively to build common learning targets. This ensures that when the students take common formative assessments, the emphasis of each lesson will have been the same, making the data produced by these assessments more reliable.

By the start of second semester, staff will have worked on their learning targets and incorporating the targets into their practice for four months. If staff are not yet proficient in writing and using targets, leaders can provide retraining and continue working toward the initial goals. If staff are ready to move on, the organization creates a new set of thirty-, sixty-, and ninety-day goals. Assume the example staff has progressed well in the first semester, and consider these example second-semester goals.

- **Thirty-day goal:** By February 6, 100 percent of learning targets will be written to support student learning in a given lesson, not behavioral expectations.

- **Sixty-day goal:** By March 13, 100 percent of lessons will begin with students being introduced to the learning target and conclude with students reviewing their progress on the stated learning target.

- **Ninety-day goal:** By April 20, during 100 percent of lessons, staff will reference the learning target at least once during instruction.

Where first semester began with staff learning about the *why* of learning targets and aligning them with their teammates, second semester has focused on more effectively writing and using the targets. If a site stays on this path, they will easily reach their teacher skill goal by the end of the year. Along the way, if staff are struggling with a thirty-day section, the next goal can be modified to provide more support.

SMART Goals

All goals, short and long term, should be written in SMART goal format. This will ensure the goals are strategic and specific, measurable, attainable, results oriented, and time bound (Conzemius & Morganti-Fisher, 2012; O'Neill & Conzemius, 2006).

- **Strategic and specific:** *Strategic* means that the goal has a purpose that will directly benefit students. *Specific* means that the phrasing of the goal eliminates vague language—there is no confusion as to the learning or skill being addressed.

- **Measurable:** The results of the goal are easily measurable. There might be a numeric scale associated or a clear *yes* or *no* on whether the team met its goal or not.

- **Attainable:** The team has the ability to achieve the goal. It may be difficult, but reaching the goal is possible. For contrast, consider an unattainable goal such as 100 percent of students reading on grade level in six months if currently only 35 percent of students can read on grade level.

- **Results oriented:** The goal prioritizes outcomes rather than activities. For example, the number of students who reach proficiency at the end of a unit is an outcome, while a teacher covering a concept in class is an activity.

- **Time bound:** The goal includes a deadline or time frame.

A word of caution: it is not uncommon to see SMART goals presented with alternative definitions. A team might want to let the *R* for *results oriented* stand for *reasonable* or *realistic* instead. Teams should resist these changes. For one thing, *reasonable* and *realistic* duplicate the meaning of the *A*, *attainable*. It's also important to retain the criterion of *results oriented* because it aligns with the third big idea of a PLC—a focus on results. This element of SMART goals helps teams stay focused on all students and the data they are producing, good, bad, or indifferent.

Celebrating Progress and Achievements

In *School Improvement for All*, Kramer and Schuhl (2017) state, "Celebrations act as an antidote to constant change. They indicate what an organization values. They shape the stories that people tell themselves" (p. 37). DuFour and colleagues (2016) concur; they maintain that celebrations reinforce "the commitments members demonstrate in day-to-day work" (p. 36). Chapter 4 (page 66) mentions that leaders can celebrate teachers' work during an observation by beginning feedback with an *I like* statement. However, celebrations should not be limited to these quick affirmations; celebrations of student learning and staff practices should be regular and planned. DuFour and colleagues (2016) remind leaders that "when celebrations continually remind people of the purpose and priorities of their organizations, members are more likely to embrace the purpose and work toward agreed-on priorities" (p. 221). These staff celebrations go a long way toward showing staff what the educational leader values. If the school only celebrates state test scores, it is those test scores that staff will pay the most attention to. If a leader celebrates student growth, the use of innovative teaching strategies, and collaboration, staff will look beyond the annual rollout of state assessment scores to find value in their students' and their own work.

These celebrations can be small or large, but they need to take place. A celebration of practice can be asking a staff member to share a best practice with the rest of the staff at a staff meeting. A larger celebration can be bringing in lunch for staff, allowing them to leave at the end of the students' dismissal on a Friday, or getting staff together at someone's house. The manner of the celebration is not that important. What is important is that it takes place.

Minda Zetlin (2014) maintains that celebrations are so important to an organization that they need to be well planned and executed in a meaningful way. Zetlin (2014) lays out four celebration strategies leaders can use to keep an organization reaching for higher achievement when it reaches small and big goals: (1) brag, (2) think back to where you started, (3) feel lucky, and (4) remember your larger goal. This process for goal setting and celebrating honors the difficult work staff are asked to do and the effort that goes into meeting the goals. By recognizing when the people who make up the organization meet goals, the *we* culture becomes more ingrained. That is why Zetlin's ideas for celebrations work very well for districts and schools. In the following sections, we'll discuss her four celebration strategies, as well as staff awards and community assemblies.

Brag

It has never been easier to let the world know about the successes of your district or school. Social media platforms like Twitter, Instagram, and Facebook allow leaders to take their messages directly to stakeholders. A post or picture showing the students who have earned the monthly behavioral award for being respectful will get great engagement (assuming the school has the appropriate permission or image release). A quick profile of a teacher celebrating the academic growth of his or her classes will create goodwill and spread the message that this professional does a great job supporting students. Kindness clubs, STEAM activities, and learning opportunities beyond the classroom are nice additions to the usual athletics and arts pictures and videos that schools share. These social media celebrations all help spread the message that this district or school is special.

Leaders can also work with traditional media through press releases. Leaders who want to share celebratory news should not overlook local media. A quick mention on the radio or a small article in the newspaper will reach hundreds or thousands, depending on the market size. Leaders should take advantage of the fact that local media is always looking for a good news story.

School leaders should also seize every opportunity to share good news with stakeholders directly, be it at a school board meeting, PTO gathering, or the supermarket. Good words from leaders, in formal or informal settings, reassure parents and staff alike. We'll discuss this further in chapter 7 (page 113).

Once a school or district has made the fundamental shift to accountable PLC, a great way to brag is to become a model professional learning community. If the school's or district's application is accepted, not only does the school receive a flag to proudly display, but also the district or site is listed on AllThingsPLC (http://allthingsplc.info) and can serve as a model for other districts and schools trying to make the same journey. Once a school becomes a model PLC, it can also apply for the prestigious DuFour Award (www.solutiontree.com/awards/dufour-award), which is awarded annually to one PLC school that demonstrates outstanding student achievement. Past winners, like Mason Crest Elementary School in Annandale, Virginia, or Fern Creek High School in Louisville, Kentucky, proudly display their trophies in ongoing celebration of students and staff.

Think Back to Where You Started

Another way to celebrate growth is simply to pause and look back on how far you've come. That moment of reflection will not only illuminate the path an organization has trod to reach where it now stands, but often shows the road that still needs to be traveled. It is important for a school to stop and say, "We had 31 percent of our students proficient in reading two years ago. Today we have 53 percent. That is a huge increase! Great job!" Although 53 percent of students in a school reaching proficiency is certainly not all, it is significantly further along than 31 percent. That kind of growth as an organization might deserve a night of staff celebration with margaritas at someone's house. This will let staff know that leadership recognizes how far the district or school has come and how hard everyone has worked to get the students to that level of proficiency. It will help inspire staff to push for 75 percent, and then 90 percent.

Leaders should seek to remind staff of their beginnings, when they did PLC lite, and how their instruction and discipline have changed since committing to becoming an accountable professional learning community. It's easy for professionals to get lost in the daily work of making collective commitments come to fruition, building common formative assessments, and analyzing the data those assessments produce; staff members need a deliberate reminder from the leader in the form of appreciation and encouragement.

Feel Lucky

There is not a day in education I do not feel lucky—lucky to be in the classroom with great students, lucky to be an administrator in schools with staff willing to learn and push their practices, and lucky to work at the district level with colleagues I learn from. You can celebrate progress simply by feeling lucky that your district or school is willing to do the difficult, collaborative work of holding all staff accountable to all students learning at grade level or higher.

Feeling lucky is a mindset; it is about gratitude—in this case, gratitude that you can do something you love to support students. Gratitude as an emotion has the power to strengthen relationships because it is social in its nature. CEO and author Camille Preston (2017) calls gratitude the sister of feedback. Preston goes on to note that gratitude carries no cost, builds internal resilience, and empowers others (Preston, 2017). Researcher Robert Emmons states that "gratitude heals, energizes, and transforms lives" (Emmons, 2020).

If you do not feel grateful, you might talk to colleagues at a different school or district who are not on the PLC journey. Often the struggles of traditional systems can help put the challenge of the PLC process in perspective. There is no denying that all teaching is hard work, but remember how far you have come from top-down leadership, isolated teaching practices, disengaged students, and so on.

Another way to feel lucky is to think back to when you were trying to get your first teaching job or interviewing to move to the next level of leadership. You may have thought about all the amazing things you would do if you could just get the opportunity. Now you have the opportunity! Feel lucky, go do amazing things, and take your colleagues with you.

Remember Your Larger Goal

Although celebrating progress and the achievement of smaller goals is essential, it's also important to recommit to the larger goal. The ultimate goal of a PLC is that all students learn at grade level or higher, and it's likely there will always be more work to do. In this sense, celebrations are also a way to stay motivated to keep going. For example, even after Desert View Elementary School had earned a 5 out of 5 on the Oregon state report card, a 10 out of 10 on www.greatschools.com, recognition as the first model PLC school in Oregon, and acknowledgement as a runner-up for the DuFour Award, staff had the perspective that there was always room for improvement. If someone had asked one of the teachers, "Are you a great school?", the teacher would have responded with an enthusiastic "not yet!" Not yet, because not every student was proficient at every learning target; not every student felt loved, supported, and challenged. Not yet because there is still an urgency to support all students and prepare all students with the skills that will make them successful later in life. It is important for an organization to maintain the mindset that you are working for that big hairy audacious goal (DuFour, 2014).

TEACHER PERSPECTIVE

Kara Frazier admitted that until Desert View began holding whole-staff celebrations and acknowledgements of all teachers, she was never really invested in the school's state assessment scores. She felt they were a reflection of third-, fourth-, or fifth-grade results and had very little to do with her as a first-grade teacher. However, when all staff became involved in celebrations of student successes, she began to feel like she owned a piece of those results, too (K. Frazier, personal communication, April 17, 2019).

Give Staff Awards

Teaching is hard. Staff need to feel like they are being appreciated for their hard work. Tim Kanold (2017), in his book *HEART!*, reminds readers that staff "need to see themselves in the narrative of our work" (p. 143). Giving staff awards is an easy way to do this. Richard DuFour, as principal of Adlai E. Stevenson High School, handed out the SuperPat award (so named because the school's mascot is the Patriot), and the celebrations became a way of creating shared purpose and a sense of belonging. Staff members could nominate any team or staff member who went above and beyond to move the school closer to its vision, values, and desired student outcomes (Kanold, 2017). Applying a rubric to an award can make it more authentic, rather than giving an award simply because it's someone's turn.

However, not all recognitions need a rubric. Desert View Elementary School handed out a monthly Hair-on-Fire Award (the trophy was a headband with a construction-paper flame taped to the top, which the winner would wear throughout the staff meeting), for which the only criterion was that the nominee had made a difference that week. Everyone was eligible to receive the award, from teachers to paraprofessionals to office staff to custodians. Each recipient would choose the next person to receive the award; the acknowledgment could be for almost any reason imaginable, such as being a great teammate, covering a duty so a staff member could attend a ceremony of recognition for her child, or going the extra mile to support a diabetic student and her mom. The lack of a rubric and the fact that the award crossed all job categories served to help build community in the school.

TEACHER PERSPECTIVE

Ashley Nicodemus noted that celebrations are a way for teachers to feel collaborative and supported in their practice. Receiving a Hair-on-Fire Award was one way of getting feedback from her colleagues. It told her that all staff were on the same page and served as a reassurance that she was doing a good job. At the end of the day, whole-school, whole-staff, or smaller celebrations were just another way for teachers to know they were not alone (A. Nicodemus, personal communication, April 28, 2019).

Hold Assemblies and Gatherings

Frequent small celebrations are important, but big celebrations after reaching goals and significant achievements are also important. Your team set a goal and reached it? Celebrate. Your school got an award? Celebrate. Hold an assembly and invite district office personnel. Invite parents. Invite the media. Invite the school board members, the mayor, and key business leaders. Get the marching band to play! If your school does not have a marching band, invite the local high school to send theirs. Make it big!

One school I worked with did just this after earning the top score on its state report card for the first time. The assembly occurred in the gym, which was packed with students and parents. School leaders gave a short explanation of how schools earn their scores on the report card, followed by a graphic featuring the locations throughout the state of the recent top-scoring schools. With this background established, students were told the year's score was about to be revealed. A random series of numbers flashed across the screen until it finally stopped at a giant 5 out of 5. The students and parents roared! Staff pulled the confetti poppers they had been concealing. Amid the rain of confetti, the students and parents were thanked for their hard work. Students were then told that because of their hard work, they had earned a milk-and-cookies party for everyone! As the students filed out, they were high-fiving and dancing—high-fiving and dancing about something that, thirty minutes prior, they'd known nothing about. The report card score became a source of pride for students and parents alike. The next night, the staff got together for their own celebration. When the adults in the building arrived at the home of one of the teachers, they encountered a three-and-a-half-foot-tall number 5 on the front lawn. Staff then enjoyed the evening of celebrating their hard work and capped it off with a group picture of all staff holding up five fingers. Big or small, celebrations ensure there is no confusion about what your organization values.

Summary

Truly shifting to a *we* culture requires teams and teams require goals. The importance of setting goals is reinforced by everyone from Coryell (2019) to DuFour (2014) to Collins (2001). A goal creates a common path for the entire team to walk together. Yearlong goals serve as a spot on the horizon to travel toward. Kramer and Schuhl (2017) recommend using thirty-, sixty-, and ninety-day goals as markers along the way to keep the team focused and on track. Leaders must remember that striving toward goals—especially long-term goals—is hard work and teams need to celebrate. When a team hits their thirty-day goal, celebrate. Sixty-day goal reached? Celebrate. Ninety-day goal achieved? Celebrate! Zetlin (2014) encourages districts and schools to celebrate when you reach a goal, brag about successes, pause to think back to where you started, and feel lucky, but always remember your larger goal and keep moving forward.

Chapter 6 Discussion Questions

1. In what areas do the data show we need to improve student learning the most? What SMART goals should we establish for the entire district or school to address these issues?

2. What support do we anticipate giving to teams so they can align their goals to support our goals? When and how can we deliver this support?

3. What is a story of a celebration you were involved in that made you feel good about your job? Tell it.

4. How can small celebrations be worked into feedback given to teachers? Does your organization have a staff acknowledgement award? If so, do people look forward to receiving the award? If not, what can you do to get one started?

5. What goal should you set as a district or school that when accomplished can be shared with all students?

Chapter 6 Reflection Worksheet

Learning Target

My job after reading this chapter is to gain an understanding of the integral part setting goals and celebrating progress play in making positive changes to an organization.

Success Criteria

▸ *I can explain why goal setting as an organization is important to its long-term growth.*

▸ *I understand the role celebrating small wins can play in improving classroom practices.*

▸ *I work with the guiding coalition to set goals for the organization and plan celebrations for the staff which will create a greater sense of community.*

I would restate the learning target for this chapter in this way:

If I had to pick one idea or concept from this chapter that really stands out, it would be:

The concept or idea that sparks my imagination is:

Those imaginative ideas are:

The success criterion that gives me the biggest challenge is:

Steps I can take to help overcome that challenge are:

Setting Yearlong Academic Goals

Collaborative team: _____

Date: _____

Select an essential standard around which to create a yearlong SMART goal:

Does the standard have relevance? Does it relate to the real world? Does it relate to other subjects?

☐ Yes   ☐ No

Does the standard have endurance? Will it come up over and over in a student's career?

☐ Yes   ☐ No

Will the standard be assessed on the year-end summative assessment?

☐ Yes   ☐ No

Does the standard have leverage? Does mastering this standard lead to understanding future concepts?

☐ Yes   ☐ No

Rationale, including past data, for selecting this standard:

To be on track to meet this goal at the end of the year, our thirty-day goal is:

Are we on track?

☐ Yes   ☐ No

If not, the actions we need to take are:

To be on track to meet this goal at the end of the year, our sixty-day goal is:

Are we on track?

☐ Yes   ☐ No

If not, the actions we need to take are:

To be on track to meet this goal at the end of the year, our ninety-day goal is:

Are we on track?

☐ Yes   ☐ No

If not, the actions we need to take are:

After meeting our ninety-day goal, we will reassess and create new thirty-, sixty-, and ninety-day goals to keep us on track toward our yearlong goal.

Shifting From Me to We © 2020 Solution Tree Press • SolutionTree.com
Visit **go.SolutionTree.com/PLCbooks** to download this free reproducible.

"What Can We Do to Help?"

*Education is a team sport, and the more
in sync the team, the better the results.*

—Karen Mapp, Ilene Carver, and Jessica Lander

As you lead the shift from an individualistic culture to a collaborative one, consider who comes to mind when this book references *we*. If you work at the district level, do you picture your cabinet and site principals? If you work at the school level, do you think of your teachers? In this chapter, I challenge you to expand your vision of *we*. The *C* in PLC stands for *community*. Imagine how powerful the PLC process can become if everyone in the community is engaged in and supporting the work of the collaborative teams. Chapter 4 (page 69) discussed the importance of including all adults on staff, not just classroom teachers. When this typically under-utilized and under-trained group of caring professionals buys into the mission, vision, and collective commitments of the organization, the work becomes easier. Now extend this concept even further. If the school board understands the power of intentionally answering the four critical questions of a PLC, how might their support

Learning Target

My job after reading this chapter is to be able to create a plan in which all adults in the community have a role in turning this organization into an accountable professional learning community.

Success Criteria

▶ I can explain to the school board the benefits to students of building an accountable professional learning community.

▶ I can plan a training for parents so they better understand and support the work the staff are putting into becoming an accountable professional learning community.

▶ I can reach out to community organizations to share my school's or district's mission with a wider audience.

change? How might parents contribute once they understand what it means when you say the goal is for all students to become proficient? What partnerships might form with local businesses and organizations if you brought them to the table? Often, once these stakeholders begin to learn about the transformative possibilities of a PLC, they ask, "What can we do to help?" By drawing these groups into the mission and vision of the district or school and informing them of the collective commitments the organization has made to ensure all students are learning at a high level, a leader will build a more powerful and energized *we*.

Communicating With the School Board

In most districts, each principal must go in front of the local school board once a year and give a presentation about his or her school. For site leaders, this mandate comes with a lot of stress. The stress stems not only from presenting to the board but from the daunting task of squeezing the metaphorical ten pounds of stuff into a five-pound bag. Schools are immensely complex systems and leaders usually have a lot of information that they are excited to share; a seven- to ten-minute presentation means the leader might need to omit or condense a lot of information. Instead of worrying about describing the entire school to the board, the campus leader can present the efforts all staff members are making to become an accountable professional learning community as a first step. Ensuring the board members understand the three big ideas and the four critical questions of a PLC will help them get behind what the school is doing. Full understanding will take more than a short presentation, so the leader will need to develop a plan to train the school board.

First, the leader needs to help board members develop understanding of the key concepts and research around professional learning communities. Key selections from resources such as *Learning by Doing* (DuFour et al., 2016), *In Praise of American Educators* (DuFour, 2015), *Taking Action: A Handbook for RTI at Work* (Buffum, Mattos, & Malone, 2018), and *School Improvement for All* (Kramer & Schuhl, 2017) can provide a fundamental understanding of what a professional learning community will look like and the expectations that will be in place for all children to learn at grade level or better.

To build the initial presentation, the leader might treat it like the annual report a business executive gives to shareholders each year. Trudie Longren, a business writer, says a CEO will share the financial health of a business, new products that may be launched, the outlook for the coming year, and information regarding research and development (Longren, 2020). Taking this as a model, the learning leader should lay out past data for the school, both good and bad. Marc Johnson, former superintendent of Sanger Unified School District in Sanger, California, notes that receiving frank assessments from the superintendent, district cabinet members, and school leaders builds understanding among board members (M. Johnson, personal communication, March 12, 2020).

It is important for the board to see data beyond the year-end state assessment. The data presented to the board should also include team-selected essential standards, SMART goals for the site and teams, common assessments (both formative and summative), and a sample of student learning data. Johnson says that, during meetings, the Sanger Unified board room was turned into a data room, with charts of student successes and challenges posted all around (M. Johnson, personal communication, March 12, 2020).

The school board should also be informed of the details of the PLC process. In this piece, the leader will explain how this work will look in his or her specific district or school. At the site level, this may include what the master schedule might look like, when intervention and extension times will be provided, and an overview of when and how the staff will be trained to effectively answer the four critical questions of a PLC. To gain the board's support, leaders should avoid vague descriptions in favor of detailed plans. Communicate about the staff's efforts to provide crystal-clear learning objectives to students, assess what students have learned, respond when students are not learning, and extend the learning once students demonstrate proficiency. In Sanger Unified, for example, leaders took board members on tours of their schools so they could see how the concepts were applied at the classroom level and how students were benefiting from them (M. Johnson, personal communication, March 12, 2020). These tours help board members not only better understand how the four critical questions drive instruction, but also realize who is affected by the decisions they make (teachers and students).

The leader should conclude the training of the board with the results that the board should expect as the organization works to become more collaborative and focused on student learning. The vast majority of people who run for a local school board want to be part of the team that helps students succeed and this understanding will help them support the district's or school's needs. If the leader seizes this presentation as an opportunity to really educate board members as to how the school is ensuring all students learn, he or she will be helping to build support for the site. In short, the leader expands his or her team beyond the building to include a group of people who can provide crucial support for the mission of ensuring all students learn.

Beyond once-a-year presentations, the leader can continue to support board members' learning by providing resources to them. The recommendations on essential standards from Buffum and colleagues (2018) in *Taking Action* would be interesting reading for board members. One of thousands of videos available on Global PD (www.GlobalPD.com) or any number of short clips on YouTube featuring PLC experts like Rick DuFour, Becky Dufour, Mike Mattos, or Robert Eaker would serve as a great starting point for these adults whose work it is to support the school. In short, the leader needs to actively educate this group in current educational theory.

Formal settings are not the only place that board members can extend their learning. Johnson suggests developing understanding and relationships with the school board by hosting an informal dinner prior to an official meeting. This type of setting creates an opportunity to make personal connections and build trust between the learning leaders and those that support the work of the district and schools (M. Johnson, personal communication, March 2020).

Board meetings are very important to the school in getting support for the journey toward operating as a professional learning community. Keller and Papasan (2013) remind readers in *The ONE Thing* that "an accountability partner will positively impact your productivity" (p. 188). So, having these accountability partners is a very positive thing. A leader of a district or school should take every opportunity to welcome their feedback and support. Another stakeholder group that serves as important accountability partners is parents, which we discuss in the next section.

Communicating With Parents

The first meeting of the year with the parent council (often called the parent-teacher organization or parent liaison committee) usually does not carry the same type of anxiety as going in front of the school board. Often the leader knows these parents well and they usually have positive things to say about the organization. These parents may volunteer frequently, and they are involved and engaged in the school and in their children's education. They are just as important to mobilize as board members. Educating these parents about the three big ideas and four critical questions will create messengers who can communicate the mission and vision to other parents. These parents are often active in other parts of the community, with baseball leagues, dance classes, the public library, and so on. They may be able to recruit resources that the leader is not even aware of.

As with board members, the leader should view active, involved parents as positive vehicles for carrying the message that this district or school will be operating differently. However, the district or school leader should not only share information with those parents who are active and involved. The leader should educate all parents about the new *we* culture of the school. The leader can take a similar approach to the presentation to parents that he or she took with the board. A short presentation from the guiding coalition will illustrate for the parents how the three big ideas and the four critical questions of a PLC will help their children. There will be no silos of teachers working independently; instead teams strive to work interdependently. A student's success in school is not dependent on the teacher to which she is assigned because she will be supported by the entire grade-level team, including elective teachers and the support personnel working with that grade. As an organization, the goal will be all students learning at grade level or better. As fundamental as those ideas seem to those of us in education, they are radical ideas to those whose K–12 experience ended the day they received their high school diplomas.

The leader should present these important messages at events such as back-to-school night and new student orientation. If there are segments of the population that typically do not come to the school, the leader might hold meetings in community locations that are more easily accessible for parents, such as the recreation room of an apartment complex, the common areas of other housing developments, or other community gathering places. By bringing the message outside the school, the leader demonstrates how important families and neighborhoods are to the success of the school.

The PLC process is very different from what most of your students' parents would have experienced in school, and sometimes this is a challenge. Education is unique as an industry in that everyone has extensive experience in it. Imagine that every customer at a local donut shop had previously worked as a donut maker—they would likely have strong opinions about the donut-making process and the resulting quality. In education, everyone has helped make donuts and the experience shapes each adult's perception of what school is and should be. Some parents will be skeptical of any school-system initiative because their own school experiences were negative. Others, who had good experiences in traditional education, will not see a reason to do anything differently than they did in their classrooms. To counteract preconceived notions, especially those born of the *select-and-sort* schools (institutions designed to rank students and separate those who can from those who cannot) that many adults attended in the past, the school leader needs to communicate clearly and compellingly about how and why a professional learning community operates differently. It is up to the leader of the district or school to educate these well-meaning, supportive parents on why the way it used to be did not address the needs of all students and how the PLC process does just that.

To overcome each adult's expectation of school for his or her child being exactly what he or she experienced as a child, the leader needs to revisit Sinek's advice and "start with why" (Sinek, 2009). By articulating the reasons and purpose for the change from teachers working in isolation to teams working interdependently, the leader will begin to gain support and buy-in from parents. Initially, it will seem counterintuitive to these school veterans to focus, as a district or school, on a few collective commitments and a few essential standards. They might ask, "What about everything else?" But when educated by the leader, these supportive adults can become advocates for the PLC process throughout the community.

There are many resources about PLCs available to leaders to guide the conversation with parents. Why not begin each PTO meeting with one of the scenarios that the authors present at the beginning of each chapter in *Learning by Doing* (DuFour et al., 2016)? Each of these case studies illustrates challenges of the PLC journey and why PLC lite does not achieve results. Similarly, the opening stories of the chapters in *Enriching the Learning* (Roberts, 2019) would prompt a lively discussion about extensions and challenges for students who have already reached proficiency. These types of stories are a great way to engage parents and help them understand the need for professional learning communities.

A parent's relationship with the classroom teachers also affects quality of communication. Stakeholders will be reticent to fully buy into the efforts of the school if they do not have good relationships with the professionals who teach their children every day. Teachers have many tools at their disposal to build these relationships. Calls home, face-to-face meetings, texts, and emails all help teachers inform and connect with parents. In addition, there are digital platforms and apps that enable teachers to easily share what is happening in class. These tools offer a way to keep a record of what each student and the class have accomplished during the year. At the end of the day, parents want to know that school staff care about their children and will treat them fairly. Parents can build up anxiety when they do not know how things are going in school. By intentionally opening the lines of communication, leaders and teachers reduce that anxiety. This creates a more effective partnership between home and school.

Communicating With the Wider Community

Though board members and parents are important stakeholders with close ties to the school, further spreading the message that high levels of learning for all students is an ongoing, critical pursuit is important. Many civic organizations are looking

---

TEACHER PERSPECTIVE

In addition to frequent calls home, face-to-face meetings, texts, and emails, Kara Frazier used the Remind app to stay in touch with parents (K. Frazier, personal communication, April 17, 2019). Ashley Nicodemus did the same with the Seesaw app (A. Nicodemus, personal communication, April 28, 2019). Both Remind and Seesaw allow parents to learn what is happening in class almost in real time. Remind is an app that allows a classroom teacher to send out information—such as reminders and handouts—directly to parents. The teacher can also share photos of individual student work with that student's parent. Seesaw also enables communication between teachers and parents. Each student has an account and the student and teacher can upload student work, journals, and short presentations. The parent receives a notification when something new is added and can view and reply to the work. This helps parents better carry out the word of the great work these teachers are doing. Mrs. Nicodemus said this was especially important in kindergarten where anxious parents were greatly relieved to see their five-year-olds happy, adjusting, and making friends during their first week of school. The apps also serve as a record of the work the students do throughout the year. Parents appreciated this because, as opposed to a traditional journal, all a parent had to do was hit a button to share his or her child's work.

---

for speakers to present on community happenings and will host a school or district leader for a breakfast meeting, luncheon, or afternoon coffee. By making slight modifications to the same presentation he or she gives to the board or parents, the leader can inform engaged local citizens about the school's or district's PLC journey. A date like this every month or two can greatly expand community support for the district or school. Figure 7.1 (page 120) shows a sample proposal to a civic organization that a leader would send out to secure a time to present.

Connecting and working with community organizations builds goodwill that comes in handy when the school or district must ask for more direct support, whether that takes the form of volunteers to enact school programs or municipal bonds and tax increases. Civic leaders and active community members might volunteer to mentor struggling students in various subjects or act as reading buddies for primary students. Often members of these organizations are business leaders who are willing to train students in career skills (such as how to fill out a job application and what to wear to an interview) or even offer internships. Members of civic organizations typically enjoy being part of the *we* that helps all students succeed.

Dear Rotary Club of Springfield,

As the Principal of Northwind Middle School, I would like to come by your meeting on Wednesday, September 16, and make a presentation about some very exciting things we are doing to meet the unique challenges of students in our community.

One of the things we are most excited about is our shift to becoming a professional learning community. This process, which involves all teachers improving their professional practice through action research, will benefit all students.

Becoming a PLC means doing education very differently from what most of you experienced during your time in the classroom and I would like to highlight those differences and the exciting results we are getting through these changes.

If the preceding date does not work for your organization, please contact me about a possible alternative date and time.

Thank you,

Mick Shrimpton

Dr. Mick Shrimpton
Principal
Northwind Middle School

Figure 7.1: Sample letter to a local organization.

Summary

Expanding your vision of *we* will bring increased support and resources for your school or district and its PLC processes. By utilizing the work of Buffum and his colleagues (2018), DuFour (2015), and Kramer and Schuhl (2017), a leader can educate the school board as to the need for the organization to transform into an accountable PLC and the processes that will occur on a school level to ensure that happens. Parents and the wider community can also provide great support to a PLC. Training parents on the work of a 21st century educational organization will help them understand not just the processes that staff are using to support their students, but also how these processes differ from what they might have experienced in school. Finally, forming relationships with local organizations enables leaders to spread their message further and build community support.

Chapter 7 Discussion Questions

1. Who needs to hear our organization's mission, vision, and collective commitments?

2. How will we educate parents about what we are trying to do? How do we address parents and other stakeholders who want school to be exactly as it was when they attended?

3. Are there social media we are not accessing or using to their fullest potential?

4. Which community groups would benefit from hearing about the great things happening in our organization?

Chapter 7 Reflection Worksheet

Learning Target

My job after reading this chapter is to be able to create a plan in which all adults in the community have a role in turning this organization into an accountable professional learning community.

Success Criteria

▸ *I can explain to the school board the benefits to students of building an accountable professional learning community.*

▸ *I can plan a training for parents so they better understand and support the work the staff are putting into becoming an accountable professional learning community.*

▸ *I can reach out to community organizations to share my school's or district's mission with a wider audience.*

I would restate the learning target for this chapter in this way:

If I had to pick one idea or concept from this chapter that really stands out, it would be:

The concept or idea that sparks my imagination is:

Those imaginative ideas are:

The success criterion that gives me the biggest challenge is:

Steps I can take to help overcome that challenge are:

Planning Sheet for Presentation to a School Board or Community Organization

Presentation medium or format:

Presenters:

Mission:

Vision:

Collective commitments:

What we are most proud of:

Data showing recent successes:

Our biggest challenge to address this year:

Epilogue

The origin of this book is the work I have done across the United States helping districts and schools become more collaborative, build professional learning communities, and meet the challenges that come with shifting a culture from *me* to *we*. The questions that form the basis of each chapter are the same ones that were frequently asked of me as a building leader, district administrator, and consultant.

As I wrote this book, I wanted to include the perspectives of teachers who had done the work at the classroom level. When I asked Melissa Purswell, a middle school teacher of boundless energy and unending love for students, about her role helping lead a PLC as a teacher and guiding coalition member, she said something that really resonated with me: before becoming a PLC, "the staff was dedicated to giving it everything they had for all students every day, but we lacked some serious direction as to *how* to make that happen" (M. Purswell, personal communication, November 30, 2019). Purswell went on to say that the staff learned that enthusiasm was not enough; they needed a plan to ensure that all students were learning.

The plan she spoke of is the systematic support all students receive when a district or school commits to the three big ideas and answers the four critical questions of a PLC (DuFour et al., 2016).

1. There will be a focus on learning.

2. A district or school will establish a collaborative culture and take collective responsibility for all students' success.

3. The organization will maintain a results orientation based on the data the students are producing.

1. What is it we want our students to know and be able to do?

2. How will we know if each student has learned it?

3. How will we respond when some students do not learn it?

4. How will we extend the learning for students who have demonstrated proficiency?

In short, the school needed to shift from thirty *me*s working very, very hard for the twenty-five students in their individual classrooms to one *we* serving 603 students.

The days of the heroic lone teacher shutting his or her door and empowering a small group of students have passed. The job is too daunting and too big for one teacher to support all students' needs. Likewise, PLC-lite behaviors such as spending collaborative time on administrative and organizational topics need to cease. Neither of these scenarios will create an experience powerful enough to ensure all students learn at high levels.

Instead, districts and schools need to revisit their mission and vision statements, eliminate flowery language, clarify why they exist, and define what they need to do to make that *why* a reality. Organizations need to make collective commitments to how they will operate to ensure all students are maximizing their academic success. The learning leader can ensure these systematic supports stay in place by making a concerted effort to accomplish the mission and vision of the district or school while holding everyone accountable to the collective commitments. This will take time— multiple school years. This year's great initiative will also be next year's great initiative and the following year's great initiative. It will require training all adults on campus, regularly spending time in classrooms, and gaining the support of the school board and the parents.

When an organization can do these things, it will have made the monumental shift from a culture of *me* to a culture of *we*. It will truly be a community of professional learners and every student will be better off for it.

References and Resources

Ainsworth, L. (2003). *Power standards: Identifying the standards that matter the most.* Boston, MA: Houghton Mifflin Harcourt.

Anthis, K. (2013). *Identity at work: Career crafting.* Accessed at https://www.psychology today.com/us/blog/who-am-i/201307/identity-work-career-crafting on March 7, 2020.

Baeder, J. (2018). *Now we're talking: 21 days to high performance instructional leadership.* Bloomington, IN: Solution Tree Press.

Buffum, A., Erkens, C., Hinman, C., Huff, S., Jessie, L. G., Martin, T. L., et al. (2008). *The collaborative administrator: Working together as a professional learning community.* Bloomington, IN: Solution Tree Press.

Buffum, A., Mattos, M., & Malone, J. (2018). *Taking action: A handbook for RTI at Work.* Bloomington, IN: Solution Tree Press.

Calderón, M. E., Trejo, M. N., Montenegro, H., Carreón, A., D'Emilio, T., Marino, J., et al. (2016). *Literacy strategies for English learners in core content secondary classrooms.* Bloomington, IN: Solution Tree Press.

Carter, L. (2007). *Total instructional alignment: From standards to student success.* Bloomington, IN: Solution Tree Press.

Collins, J. (2001). *Good to great: Why some companies make the leap . . . and others don't.* New York: HarperCollins.

Conzemius, A. E., & Morganti-Fisher, T. (2012). *More than a SMART goal.* Bloomington, IN: Solution Tree Press.

Coryell, E. (2019). *Revolutionize teamwork: How to create and lead accountable teams.* Naperville, IL: Sourcebooks.

Cruz, L. (2018, October 16–18). *Why the urgency to eliminate the achievement gap for Latino and Hispanic students?* Presentation at the Solution Tree Soluciones Institute, City of Industry, CA.

Dalio, R. (2017). *Principles.* New York: Simon & Schuster.

Donohoo, J. (2017). *Collective efficacy: How educators' beliefs impact student learning.* Thousand Oaks, CA: Corwin Press.

DuFour, R. (2014, September 24–26). *First things first: Building the solid foundation of a Professional Learning Community at Work.* Presentation at the Solution Tree PLC at Work Institute, Anaheim, CA.

DuFour, R. (2015). *In praise of American educators: And how they can become even better.* Bloomington, IN: Solution Tree Press.

DuFour, R., & DuFour, R. (2014, September 24–26). *Building the collaborative culture of a Professional Learning Community at Work.* Presentation at the Solution Tree PLC at Work Institute, Anaheim, CA.

DuFour, R., DuFour, R., & Eaker, R. (2008). *Revisiting Professional Learning Communities at Work: New insights for improving schools.* Bloomington, IN: Solution Tree Press.

DuFour, R., DuFour, R., Eaker, R., & Karhanek, G. (2004). *Whatever it takes: How professional learning communities respond when kids don't learn.* Bloomington, IN: Solution Tree Press.

DuFour, R., DuFour, R., Eaker, R., Many, T. W., & Mattos, M. (2016). *Learning by doing: A handbook for Professional Learning Communities at Work* (3rd ed.). Bloomington, IN: Solution Tree Press.

DuFour, R., & Eaker, R. (1998). *Professional Learning Communities at Work: Best practices for enhancing student achievement.* Bloomington, IN: Solution Tree Press.

DuFour, R., & Fullan, M. (2013). *Cultures built to last: Systemic PLCs at Work.* Bloomington, IN: Solution Tree Press.

DuFour, R., & Marzano, R. J. (2011). *Leaders of learning: How district, school, and classroom leaders improve student achievement.* Bloomington, IN: Solution Tree Press.

DuFour, R., & Reeves, D. (2016). The futility of PLC lite. *Phi Delta Kappan, 97*(6), 69–71.

Eaker, R., & Keating, J. (2012). *Every school, every team, every classroom: District leadership for growing Professional Learning Communities at Work.* Bloomington, IN: Solution Tree Press.

Emmons, R. (2020). *Gratitude works.* Accessed at https://emmons.faculty.ucdavis.edu/ on March 10, 2020.

Fowler, S. (2017). *Why motivating people doesn't work . . . and what does: The new science of leading, energizing, and engaging.* San Francisco: Berrett-Koehler Publishers.

Gordon, J. (2017). *The power of positive leadership: How and why positive leaders transform teams and organizations and change the world.* Hoboken, NJ: Wiley.

Gordon, J., & Smith, M. (2015). *You win in the locker room first: The 7 C's to build a winning team in business, sports, and life.* Hoboken, NJ: Wiley.

Halford, G., Baker, R., McCredden, J., & Bain, J. (2005). How many variables can humans process? *Psychological Science, 16*(1), 70–76. Accessed at https://journals .sagepub.com/doi/abs/10.1111/j.0956-7976.2005.00782.x on January 17, 2020.

Hattangadi, V. (2016). Unfreeze-change-refreeze. Accessed at www.drvidyahattangadi .com/unfreeze-change-freeze on November 25, 2019.

Hattie, J. (2009). *Visible learning: A synthesis of over 800 meta-analyses relating to achievement.* New York: Routledge.

Hattie, J. (2019). *The* Visible Learning *research.* Accessed at https://www.visiblelearning plus.com/content/visible-learning-research on December 30, 2019.

Heath, C., & Heath, D. (2008). *Made to stick: Why some ideas survive and others die.* New York: Random House.

Holtzclaw, E. (2012). The power of consistency: 5 rules. *Inc.* Accessed at https://www.inc .com/eric-v-holtzclaw/consistency-power-success-rules.html on March 15, 2020.

Iger, R. (2019). *The ride of a lifetime: Lessons learned from 15 years as CEO of the Walt Disney Company.* New York: Random House.

Kanold, T. D. (2017). *Heart! Fully forming your professional life as a teacher and leader.* Bloomington, IN: Solution Tree Press.

Keating, J., Brown, T., Cruz, L., Leane, B., Mattos, M., Nielsen, M., & Roberts, M. (2019, August). *PLC at Work panel discussion.* Panel discussion conducted at the Solution Tree Professional Learning Community at Work Institute, Detroit, MI.

Keller, G., & Papasan, J. (2013). *The ONE thing: The surprisingly simple truth behind extraordinary results.* Austin, TX: Bard Press.

Kokemuller, N. (n.d.). *The effects of team commitment.* Accessed at http://smallbusiness .chron.com/effects-team-commitment-42028.html on November 25, 2019.

Kotter, J. (2014). *Accelerate.* Boston, MA: Harvard Business School Publishing.

Kotter, J. P., & Cohen, D. S. (2002). *The heart of change: Real-life stories of how people change their organizations.* Boston, MA: Harvard Business Review Press.

Kouzes, J. M., & Posner, B. Z. (2010). *The truth about leadership: The no-fads, heart-of-the-matter facts you need to know.* San Francisco: Jossey-Bass.

Kramer, S. V., & Schuhl, S. (2017). *School improvement for all: A how-to guide for doing the right work.* Bloomington, IN: Solution Tree Press.

Kurtz, G. (producer), & Kershner, I. (director). (1980). *The empire strikes back* [Motion picture]. United States: Lucasfilm.

LaMonte, B., & Shook, R. L. (2004). *Winning the NFL way: Leadership lessons from football's top head coaches.* New York: HarperCollins.

Lapowsky, I. (2014, January 28). The most important person in your office isn't who you think. *Inc.* Accessed at www.inc.com/issie-lapowsky/the-most-important-person-in -the-office.html on November 25, 2019.

Lewin, K. (1947). Frontiers in group dynamics: Concept, method and reality in social science; equilibrium and social change. *Human Relations, 1*(1), 5–41.

Li, C. (2019). *The disruption mindset: Why some organizations transform while others fail.* Oakton, VA: Ideapress Publishing.

Longren, T (2020). What goes into a stockholder's report. Accessed at https://smallbusiness.chron.com/goes-stockholders-report-65606.html on January 30, 2020.

Mapp, K. L., Carver, I., & Lander, J. (2017). *Powerful partnerships: A teacher's guide to engaging families for student success.* New York: Scholastic.

McKeown, G. (2014). *Essentialism: The disciplined pursuit of less.* New York: Crown Business.

Muhammad, A. (2018). *Transforming school culture: How to overcome staff division* (2nd ed.). Bloomington, IN: Solution Tree Press.

Muhammad, A., & Cruz, L. F. (2019). *Time for change: Four essential skills for transformational school and district leaders.* Bloomington, IN: Solution Tree Press.

National Governors Association Center for Best Practices & Council of Chief State School Officers. (2010). *Common Core State Standards for English language arts and literacy in history/social studies, science, and technical subjects.* Washington, DC: Authors.

Nordhall, O., & Knez, I. (2018). Motivation and justice at work: The role of emotion and cognition components of personal and collective work identity. *Frontiers in Psychology.* Accessed at https://www.frontiersin.org/articles/10.3389/fpsyg.2017.02307/full on January 29, 2020.

O'Neill, J., & Conzemius, A. (2006) *The power of SMART goals: Using goals to improve student learning.* Bloomington, IN: Solution Tree Press.

Oregon Department of Education Quality Education Commission. (2018). *Quality education model: Final report.* Salem, OR: Author.

Preston, C. (2017). Why expressing gratitude is good for business and people. *Forbes.* Accessed at https://www.forbes.com/sites/forbescoachescouncil/2017/11/09/why -expressing-gratitude-is-good-for-business-and-people/#1d5be3cd6eca on March 10, 2020.

Roberts, M. (2019). *Enriching the learning: Meaningful extensions for proficient students in a PLC at Work.* Bloomington, IN: Solution Tree Press.

Roth, D. (2013). Supporting healthy conflict in the workplace. *Forbes.* Accessed at https://www.forbes.com/sites/davidroth/2013/07/29/supporting-healthy-conflict-in-the -workplace/#537618d91822 on March 7, 2020.

Rotter, J. B. (1954). *Social learning and clinical psychology.* Upper Saddle River, NJ: Prentice-Hall.

Shim, J. (2013). Involving the parents of English language learners in a rural area: Focus on the dynamics of parent-teacher interactions. *Rural Educator, 34*(3), 18–26. Accessed at https://journals.library.msstate.edu/index.php/ruraled/article/view /396/364 on March 6, 2020.

Sinek, S. (2009) *Start with why: How great leaders inspire everyone to take action.* New York: Portfolio.

Spiller, J., & Power, K. (2019). *Leading with intention: Eight areas for reflection and planning in your PLC at Work.* Bloomington, IN: Solution Tree Press.

Stiggins, R. J. (2011, September). *The role of grades in the standards-driven schools of the 21st century*. Presentation at 6th Annual Sound Grading Practices Conference in Portland, OR.

Stiggins, R. J., Arter, J. A., Chappuis, J., & Chappuis, S. (2004). *Classroom assessment for student learning: Doing it right—using it well*. Portland, OR: Assessment Training Institute.

Stone, D., & Heen, S. (2014). *Thanks for the feedback: The science and art of receiving feedback well*. New York: Penguin Books.

TEDx Talks. (2009, September). Start with why—how great leaders inspire action | Simon Sinek | TEDxPugetSound [Video file]. Accessed at www.youtube.com /watch?v=u4ZoJKF_VuA on January 29, 2020.

Tredgold, G. (2017, December 6). *4 unexpected benefits of increasing focus*. Accessed at www.huffpost.com/entry/4-unexpected-benefits-of-incresing-focus_b_9458556 on November 25, 2019.

Williams, K. C., & Hierck, T. (2015). *Starting a movement: Building culture from the inside out in professional learning communities*. Bloomington, IN: Solution Tree Press.

Zetlin, M. (2014, April 8). Why you must celebrate small successes. *Inc.* Accessed at www .inc.com/minda-zetlin/why-you-must-celebrate-small-successes.html on November 25, 2019.

Ziglar, Z. (2019). *Goals: How to get the most out of your life*. Shippensburg, PA: Sound Wisdom.

Index

Professional Learning Communities at Work® and High Reliability Schools™
Edited by Robert Eaker and Robert J. Marzano

Dramatically improve schooling by harnessing the collective power of the High Reliability Schools™ (HRS) model and the PLC at Work® process. Featuring some of America's best educators, this anthology includes information, insights, and practical suggestions for both PLCs and HRS.

BKF938

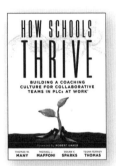

How Schools Thrive
Thomas W. Many, Michael J. Maffoni, Susan K. Sparks, and Tesha Ferriby Thomas

A companion to *Amplify Your Impact*, this resource drills deeper into the more complex aspects of PLC at Work®. Coaches and leaders will acquire new insights and strategies for improving their team's professional practice around the essential elements of the PLC process.

BKF855

Inside PLCs at Work®
Casey Reason and Craig Dougherty

Inside PLCs at Work® takes readers to Sheridan County School District 2 in Wyoming, a district that has built a PLC to great success. Using Sheridan as a real-world example, the authors prepare educators to implement the PLC process successfully in their own schools.

BKF849

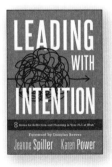

Leading With Intention
Jeanne Spiller and Karen Power

Designed as a guide and reflective tool, *Leading With Intention* will help focus your invaluable everyday work as a school leader. Discover actionable steps for creating a highly effective school community in which staff collaborate, make evidence-based decisions, and believe students are the top priority.

BKF829

"Tremendous, tremendous, tremendous!

The speaker made me do some very deep internal reflection about the **PLC process** and the personal responsibility I have in making the school improvement process work **for ALL kids.**"

—Marc Rodriguez, teacher effectiveness coach, Denver Public Schools, Colorado

PD Services

Our experts draw from decades of research and their own experiences to bring you practical strategies for building and sustaining a high-performing PLC. You can choose from a range of customizable services, from a one-day overview to a multiyear process.

Book your PLC PD today!
888.763.9045

Solution Tree